GOLGOTHA AND THE CHURCH
OF THE HOLY SEPULCHRE

GOLGOTHA AND THE CHURCH OF THE HOLY SEPULCHRE

ANDRÉ PARROT

Curator-in-Chief of the French National Museums,
Professor at the Ecole du Louvre, Paris,
Director of the Mari Archaeological Expedition

PHILOSOPHICAL LIBRARY

NEW YORK

Translated by Edwin Hudson
from the French
GOLGOTHA ET SAINT-SÉPULCRE
(Delachaux et Niestlé, Neuchâtel, 1955)

Published 1957, by the Philosophical Library, Inc.,
15 East 40th Street, New York, 16, N.Y.

All rights reserved

*Printed in Great Britain for Philosophical Library, Inc., by
The Bowering Press, Plymouth*

CONTENTS

[5]

LIST OF ILLUSTRATIONS

[7]

Illustrations

Illustrations

FOREWORD

The Church of the Holy Sepulchre is the name given to the religious building having its origin in the time of Constantine (fourth century A.D.) which covers the traditional sites of our Lord's crucifixion and burial. There are few problems of biblical archaeology more complex, for the soil of scarcely any other ancient city can have had piled upon it such a jumble of buildings. It has required all the skill of the specialist in the architecture of antiquity to disentangle them chronologically.

It is a fact that the specialists have generally come to agree with the traditional view, whether they have been Catholics, Protestants, or agnostics—and there is no reason to suppose that they have been moved by anything other than a genuine concern for the truth, uninfluenced by doctrinal considerations.

Others, who were or are sincerely religious men, have been unable to bring themselves to seek 'the living' beneath the modern marble of an edicule which is an affront to architecture and to the most elementary canons of good taste—I refer to the 'kiosk' which stands to-day on the site of the sepulchre —and they have sought and been satisfied elsewhere, for example at the 'Garden Tomb'.

Whom are we to believe—the archaeologists or these well-meaning men? To the latter, the Church of the Holy Sepulchre has often seemed impossible, not so much because it appeared to them to be 'in the middle of the town', as because of the confessional rivalries which have there been given free rein. It is easy to understand how sensitive people eventually found the perpetual squabbling around the altars intolerable, so that sincere pilgrims to the sources of their faith wished to get away from this evil atmosphere, and find some peaceful corner where they might breathe a fresher air. But that is not the point. Our task is to solve a problem of biblical topography, to locate precisely a certain site. That is a matter which ought to be decided dispassionately, in a determined spirit of complete objectivity.

It ought however to be said at the outset that this is a problem which may never be solved with certainty, that we may have to content ourselves with a high degree of probability. There is of course always a clear margin between probability and certainty. I do not believe that in this case it is possible to eliminate it. Happily, our Faith does not depend upon the assurance with which we establish or believe in the accuracy of certain Palestinian sitings. The memory of Jesus is not tied only to a few fixed points. Nevertheless it is not for the believer a matter of indifference that he should one day find himself gazing on what might in all probability be the very imprint of the feet of Him who trod the soil of Jerusalem, and who was given, on the evening of the first Good Friday, the cold stone slab of a Jewish tomb on which to 'lay His head'.

I

THE ARCHAEOLOGICAL PROBLEM
OF THE HOLY SEPULCHRE

That there is a 'problem', no one denies; but before
attempting to suggest or accept a solution it is advisable to define the problem as clearly as possible. If
the traditional site is to be defended, it must answer
the essential requirement of being outside the city as
it was in the time of our Lord. We know that He was
crucified outside Jerusalem,[1] probably not far from
a gate,[2] and doubtless near a road.[3] The place of
execution was known at the time by the name of
Golgotha, or the 'Skull'.[4] There were a garden and
a tomb there.[5]

[1] 'The place where Jesus was crucified was *nigh to the city*' (John
19.20).
[2] 'Wherefore Jesus . . . *suffered without the gate* [of the city]' (Heb.
13.12).
[3] 'And they that *passed by* railed on him' (Mark 15.29; Matt.
27.39).
[4] 'And he bearing his cross went forth into a place called *the place
of a skull*, which is called in the Hebrew *Golgotha*: where they crucified
him' (John 19.17–18).
[5] 'Now *in the place* where he was crucified there was a *garden*; and
in the garden a new *sepulchre*, wherein was never man yet laid'
(John 19.41).

These details limit the problem. Is the traditional site outside the boundary of the city of our Lord's time? Can we say that there was a gate in that sector? Were gardens and tombs located there? Is it possible to answer this threefold question in the affirmative? This is what we must now briefly examine.

*   *   *

The walls of Jerusalem.[1] In the account he gives of the siege of Jerusalem by the army of Titus (A.D. 70), the Jewish historian Josephus describes how the Romans took one after another the *three* walls of the city. Jerusalem was not in fact enclosed by three concentric defensive walls. It was only on the northern side that the city was thus defended in depth by a threefold barrier (fig. I). These defences are usually termed, in the archaeology of Jerusalem, the 'first', 'second', and 'third' walls. Only the first two were in existence in the time of Christ, the last having been built only in A.D. 41–4 by Herod Agrippa, and then only incompletely, as I shall indicate later. The course of the second and third walls must therefore be traced as precisely as possible, since *whatever the circumstances*, the site of Calvary and of the Holy Sepulchre, if they are to be valid—I do not say certain—must be between those walls. As can well

[1] An exhaustive study of the subject will be found in L. H. Vincent, *Jérusalem de l'Ancien Testament*, I, Paris, 1954, pp. 51–174 (hereinafter quoted as *JAT*).

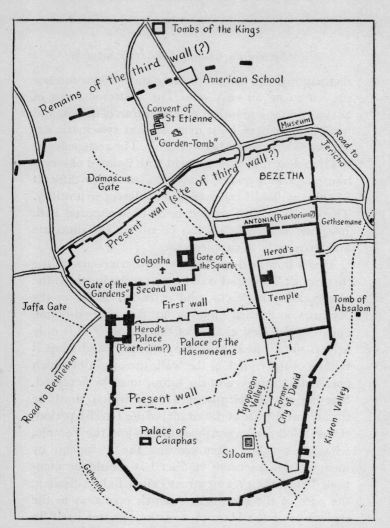

Tombs of the Kings

Remains of the third wall (?)

American School

Convent of St Etienne

"Garden-Tomb"

Museum

Road to Jericho

Damascus Gate

Present wall (site of third wall ?)

BEZETHA

ANTONIA (Praetorium?)

Gethsemane

Golgotha

Gate of the Square

Herod's

"Gate of the Gardens"

Second wall

Temple

First wall

Jaffa Gate

Herod's Palace (Praetorium?)

Palace of the Hasmoneans

Tomb of Absalom

Road to Bethlehem

Present wall

Tyropoeon Valley

Former City of David

Kidron Valley

Palace of Caiaphas

Siloam

Gehenna

I. *Jerusalem and its walls (after the plan drawn up by Fr Vincent for A. D. Sertillanges,* Ce que Jésus voyait du haut de la Croix)

be imagined, the task of plotting their course has not proved to be an easy one. The shattered ruins of ancient Jerusalem lie buried under tons of debris, and have largely been built over, so that systematic excavations have never been possible. The archaeologist has therefore had to be content with isolated observations at various points, his work made more difficult by evident ill-will and even more or less open hostility. The evidence thus gained must be compared with Josephus' text, which it has been found to illustrate and frequently to supplement.

This is how he describes the northern course of the 'first wall': 'Now that wall began on the north, at the tower called Hippicus, and extended as far as the Xystus,[1] and then, joining at the council-house, ended at the west cloister of the temple.'[2] It is only a brief note, but it raises no difficulty, and what it tells us of the course of the wall, the origin of which goes back to the era of the kings, must be accepted. Starting at the Hippicus Tower, which must be situated at the site of the citadel of the Turkish period, the wall followed a west-east axis to join the Temple, which it reached after crossing the Tyropeon by means of an imposing viaduct.[3] It should be mentioned that the present street called Bab es-Silsileh, the gate of the same name which opens on to the esplanade of the Haram, and the minaret itself 'in

---

[1] The Xystus was a court set aside for athletic games.
[2] *Jewish War*, Bk. V, 4.2.   [3] Details in *JAT*, I, pp. 51–64.

fact bear witness to the course of the old rampart, the site of the bastion which covered its junction with the original forecourt of the sanctuary, and the position of the gate to which the ancient viaduct led after the Herodian extension of the sacred enclosure.'[1]

*   *   *

The reference by Josephus to the 'second wall' is no fuller. He expresses himself in the following terms: 'The second wall took its beginning from that gate which they called "Gennath", which belonged to the first wall; it only encompassed the northern quarter of the city, and reached as far as the tower Antonia.'[2] This note gives precise information concerning only the beginning and end of the wall—the Gennath gate and the Fortress of Antonia respectively. While the latter is quite certainly to be situated at the N.W. corner of the Haram, the former is less easy to place. There is in fact no other mention of a 'Gate of the Gardens' (Gennath). In this sector, protected by a wall since the time of the kings of Judah (eighth century B.C.), the only gates known are that of Ephraim (or the Gate of the Square) and the Corner Gate.[3] There is good ground for thinking that the name was meant to have reference to a sector

[1] *JAT*, I, p. 64.
[2] *Op. cit.*, V, 4.2.
[3] II Kings 14.13; II Chronicles 25.23. The 'corner gate' is no doubt to be identified with the 'valley gate' of Nehemiah 2.13 and 3.13.

extra muros characterized by 'gardens',[1] that is to say an area not built-up, planted with trees, and certainly partially occupied by tombs cut in the rock.[2] There is however every reason to believe that this 'gate of the gardens' corresponds to the 'corner gate' of the Scriptures, and that it is to be sought not far from the Hippicus Tower,[3] and therefore in the immediate neighbourhood of the present Jaffa Gate.

It is certainly much more difficult to follow on a map of modern Jerusalem the 'second wall', between the Hippicus Tower and the Fortress of Antonia. The term κυκλούμενον, employed by Josephus, has suggested to some that the wall followed an arc between these two points.[4] But that is doubtless too rigid an interpretation of an expression that was not meant to be taken so literally. Moreover, it would be difficult to envisage a defensive line as theoretical as that, bearing no relation with reality, that is to say with the most elementary notions of city defence, as also with the lie of the land.

There are also to be taken into account a number

[1] We may recall here the mention of the 'garden' in John 19.41.

[2] Apart from those still visible in the interior of the Church of the Holy Sepulchre, with which I shall deal later, mention may be made of the hypogeum of the Herods and the necropolis on the western edge of the er-Rabâby ravine. See *JAT*, I, pp. 342–6.

[3] *Ibid.*, pp. 93–4.

[4] So *The Westminster Historical Atlas to the Bible*, Plate XVII, B, with a distended arc which puts the Church of the Holy Sepulchre inside the town, a conclusion which makes its authenticity *ipso facto* impossible.

of discoveries which, though isolated in themselves, become significant when carefully recorded on a plan of the city. Thus, fragments of wall which have come to light in the course of works of construction or reconstruction present alignments which cannot be attributed to chance,[1] and which mark out a course that leaves the Church of the Holy Sepulchre quite

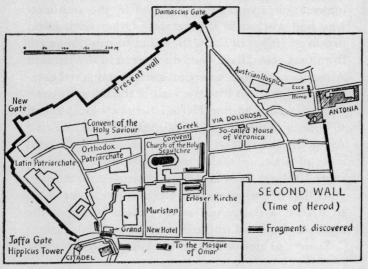

11. *The second wall (after Frs Vincent and Stève, JAT, Plates XXIV and XXIV bis)*

definitely outside the city (fig. II). At the spot where now stands the German Lutheran Church, the Erlöserkirche, the wall, after having followed a west-

[1] A detailed account of the finds is given in *JAT*, I, pp. 96–108.

[21]

east course for over two hundred yards, turns abruptly due north. In 1898, Wilhelm II, who presided at the dedication of the building, made reference to 'the considerable interest of the fact that the altar of the rebuilt church stood on the actual rampart of the city of Christ's day'.[1] It is obvious that an assertion of this sort must have been based on authoritative information, namely that supplied by the architects who had worked in that sector.[2] Other no less impressive vestiges of the wall, found to run due north from that point, have been discovered in the Russian Alexander Hospice, where an ancient staggered gateway was found let into the wall of the old rampart,[3] while a section in fine Herodian stone blocks is still to be seen in the storeroom of a *suk* in Khan ez-Zeit.[4] Altogether one is given the impression of a powerful mass of masonry which might well be a tower or, more likely, a bastion, whose position at once suggests that its purpose was to cover a gate and to help to defend a dangerous sector which included the right-angled bend in the line of the wall.[5]

Some 140 metres beyond the Erlöserkirche, where

[1] Quoted by Vincent, *ibid.*, p. 103, referring to the report published in 1899, *Das deutsche Kaiserpaar im Heiligen Land*, p. 182.

[2] Dalman, who was director of the German Archaeological Institute in Jerusalem, was however never allowed to see the plans (see G. H. Dalman, *Sacred Sites and Ways*, translated by P. P. Levertoff, S.P.C.K., London, 1935, p. 376).

[3] *JAT*, I, Plate XXV. I shall return to the point later.

[4] I myself saw this section several times in the course of my visits to Jerusalem in 1927 and 1928.   [5] *JAT*, I, p. 107.

as we have seen the line of the wall turned north, it must have borne once again to the east to link up with the Antonia fortress. The archaeological data are much more scanty in this part, and any suggestion as to the actual line of the wall can only be hypo-thetical,[1] relying more on the lie of the land than on the architectural remains, which are rare and not datable with certainty. In any case the importance of this is for our present purpose only of the slightest since it is a long way from the Church of the Holy Sepulchre.

To sum up, I consider that all the archaeological evidence points to the existence of a coherent line agreeing perfectly with the description given by Josephus. Such a line, moreover, answers very closely the military requirements of the day.[2] The 'second wall', therefore, indisputably leaves Golgotha and the site of the Church of the Holy Sepulchre outside the Jerusalem of the time of Jesus.[3]

* * *

As already stated, we owe the third rampart to Herod Agrippa I (A.D. 41–4). Josephus has this to

[1] The same perplexity is evident in the plans drawn up by all the specialists, whoever they may be. Cf., for example, *JAT*, I, Plates XXIV and XXIV *bis*.

[2] This aspect of the problem has been studied by a British officer, Capt. C. T. Morris: 'New Reasoning concerning the Fortification of Jerusalem in the First Century A.D.', in *PEQ*, 1946, pp. 19–37.

[3] G. Dalman, *op. cit.*, p. 270, gives a more systematic plan of the wall, according to which Golgotha is similarly outside the city.

say about it: 'The beginning of the third wall was at the tower Hippicus, whence it reached as far as the north quarter of the city, and the tower Psephinus, and then was so far extended till it came over against the monuments of Helena, which Helena was queen of Adiabene, the daughter of Izates: it then extended farther to a great length, and passed by the sepulchral caverns of the kings, and bent again at the tower of the corner, at the monument which is called the "Monument of the Fuller", and joined to the old wall at the valley called the "Valley of Kidron".'[1]

As a matter of fact the Jewish monarch[2] was not able to complete his project, and Josephus gives divergent explanations as to why the work was interruped. Was the king denounced in Rome by the governor of Syria, and compelled to call a halt to the construction? Or did he himself take the initiative in stopping the work, fearing to arouse the displeasure of the emperor Claudius? Or, again, was the real reason the death of the king after a few short years on the throne? What is certain is that this massive and well-constructed wall remained unfinished until the time of the insurrection, when the Jews hastened to increase its height in order to be able to use it against the Romans. The latter, however, succeeded in taking it, not by means of a frontal assault, but

[1] *Op cit.*, Book V, 4.2.
[2] He was the Herod of Acts 12.1, the grandson of Herod the Great, mentioned in Matt. 2.1.

by throwing in their attack at a point whose weakness was at once apparent—where the rampart joined the second wall. This was at its western end, in the Hippicus sector, near the so-called Gate of the Gardens.

Josephus describes the course of the wall with reference to a series of landmarks which in his own day would be known to all, so that his readers would have no difficulty in locating them. The same cannot be said to-day, since apart from the monument of Helena,[1] which in all likelihood is to be identified with the 'Tombs of the Kings', the points through which the defensive line passed—the site of the Psephinus tower, the corner tower, the Fuller's monument—are still subjects for conjecture.

Two irreconcilable theories have been put forward. The first is that of Fr Vincent, in whose opinion Agrippa's wall 'generally corresponds with the course of the present north wall',[2] that is to say the wall which is visible to-day (fig. III) and through which one passes by means of three gates: the New Gate, the Damascus Gate, and Herod's Gate. According to this theory, ruins found at the north-west corner, at the Qasr Jalud, would be those of the Psephinus tower,[3] and the 'caverns of the kings'

---

[1] A distance of 3 stadia (185 m. × 3 = 555 m.) from the rampart, according to Josephus, *Antiquities*, XX, IV, 3.95. According to either hypothesis (Vincent or Sukenik-Mayer, see below) regarding the site of the wall, the figure is inaccurate, or at best a rough approximation.
[2] *JAT*, I, p. 145.   [3] *Ibid.*, pp. 123–6, Plates XXVI–XXVII.

would be identifiable with the area of quarries near the Damascus Gate, from which much-prized stone must have been extracted.[1] At the north-east corner the wall would have bent back in a south-south-easterly direction, finishing at the corner of the Haram, i.e. the Temple.

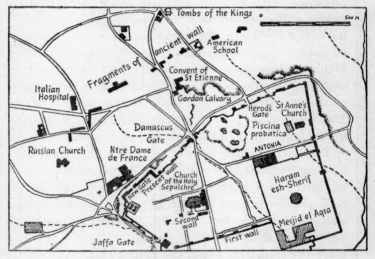

III. *The third wall* (ibid., *Plate XXXI*)

According to the second theory Agrippa's wall stood very much further north, in the area where the Italian hospital now stands. This more extended course was first suggested in 1838 by Edward Robin-

---

[1] *Ibid.*, p. 134. A certain limestone still receives the epithet *malaky* (royal).

son,[1] and was put forward again by the Americans Selah Merril and L. B. Paton. It had found little credit among modern archaeologists until a fortuitous discovery made in 1924 caused a succession of exploratory soundings to be made between 1925 and 1941. These, directed by Sukenik and Mayer, revealed a defensive line, albeit of somewhat mediocre appearance, forming a prolongation of the 'Robinson rampart' and extending to a total length of some 800 metres.[2] The excavators seem to have gained for their thesis the support of the majority of Palestinian archaeologists. They hold that these are the remains of Agrippa's rampart, referred to by Josephus as the 'third wall'. According to them, the ancient stone blocks located under the present wall of Suleiman, and particularly in the sector near the Damascus Gate, probably form part of building works carried out by Hadrian's architects in the Aelia Capitolina period, or are of even later date (third-fourth centuries A.D.).[3] Fr Vincent has disputed this interpreta-

[1] E. Robinson, *Biblical Researches in Palestine*, I (1841), pp. 314–15.

[2] E. L. Sukenik and L. A. Mayer, 'The Third Wall of Jerusalem. An Account of Excavations; A New Section of the Third Wall', in *PEQ*, 1944, pp. 145–51; W. Albright, 'New Light on the Walls of Jerusalem in the New Testament Age', in *BASOR*, 83 (1941), pp. 4–7; M. Solomiac, 'The Towers and Cisterns of the Third Wall of Jerusalem', in *BASOR*, 84 (1941), pp. 5–7; 'The Northwest Line of the Third Wall of Jerusalem', in *BASOR*, 89 (1943), pp. 18–21; Vincent, 'Autour d'un rempart mouvant', in *JAT*, I, pp. 146–70.

[3] This follows upon an excavation carried out by R. W. Hamilton, in 1937–8; see 'Excavations against the North Wall of Jerusalem', in *QDAP*, X (1940), pp. 1–53.

tion,[1] explaining the new line that came to light
between 1925 and 1941 as being a 'wall constructed
in haste' by the insurgents of the Second Revolt,
A.D. 131–5.[2] For my own part, I cannot but confess
my perplexity in face of views as categorical as they
are contradictory, expressed in each case by proven
experts who have only one interest—that of seeking
historical truth. However, whichever opinion pre-
vails, it does not bear upon the problem of the Church
of the Holy Sepulchre, the authenticity of which
depends solely upon the course of the 'second wall'.
Nevertheless I felt it right, while dealing, albeit
briefly, with the subject of the walls, to outline the
present state of the problem.

* * *

The gates in the second wall. I said above that it seems
that if Jesus was crucified outside the town, beyond
the wall therefore, it was probably not far from a
gate. In any case He must have passed through a
gate. What do we know of the gates in the second
wall, at least on the northern side of Jerusalem, which
alone concerns us here? The Scriptures do not give
us a detailed description of the walls of the city, but
there are scattered references which, with the help
of information furnished by Josephus, do nevertheless

[1] L. H. Vincent, 'Encore la troisième enceinte de Jérusalem', in
RB, 1947, pp. 90–126; *JAT*, I, pp. 129–34.
[2] See also the article 'Jérusalem' in *Dictionnaire de la Bible, Supplément*, XXI, col. 959–65.

give us some idea of the physiognomy of the northern part of the capital. In the time of the kings of Judah, and before the exile, it became necessary to take account of the continual northward spread of dwellings beyond the first wall, an extension which was natural enough given the topography of the area. There was a 'second part'[1] which Hezekiah (716–687 B.C.) protected against the Assyrian threat by means of a wall[2] which I identify with the 'second wall'. All this defensive work proved fruitless against the soldiers of Nebuchadnezzar, and the city was taken (586 B.C.) and destroyed. Nevertheless even amid this desolation the prophet Jeremiah received the assurance that 'from the tower of Hananeel unto the gate of the corner' the city would be rebuilt.[3] 'From the tower of Hananeel to the corner gate'— those were the points at the two ends of the second wall. We know that this line could be crossed through several gates.

Mention of them is made by Nehemiah, actually in connection with the work of restoration of the wall of Jerusalem, which work was authorized by the Achaemenid ruler Artaxerxes I (465–24 B.C.), whose liberal policy could afford to be generously applied to the Jews, who in the circumstances no longer constituted a threat to the greatest oriental empire of

[1] II Kings 22.14 (marg.); II Chronicles 34.22 (marg.).
[2] II Chronicles 32.5.
[3] Jeremiah 31.38.

the day. Nehemiah has provided us with a detailed topographical list in connection with his reconnaissance of the ruined wall, its reconstruction, and its dedication. These lists give us information concerning the matter in question,[1] although this is not to say that everything is thereby made perfectly clear.

The following is the relevant information, from each source:

Nehemiah 3.1–13 Reconstruction	Nehemiah 12.38–39 Dedication
	39. Prison *gate*
1. Sheep *gate*	39. Sheep *gate*
1. Tower of Meah ('the hundred')	39. Tower of Meah ('the hundred')
1. Tower of Hananeel	39. Tower of Hananeel
3. Fish *gate*	39. Fish *gate*
6. *Gate* of the Yeshana (=old)	39. *Gate* of the Yeshana (=old)
	39. *Gate* of Ephraim
8. The 'broad wall' (or wall of the square, according to Vincent)	38. The 'broad wall' (or wall of the square)
11. Tower of the furnaces	38. Tower of the furnaces
13. Valley *gate*	

One notes at once a difference in the terminology used by the various authors. The 'corner gate', well

[1] M. Burrows, 'Nehemiah 3. 1–32, as a Source for the Topography of Ancient Jerusalem', in *AASOR* (1934), pp. 115–40; 'The Topography of Nehemiah, XII, 31–43', in *JBL*, LIV (1935), p. 29f; *JAT*, I, pp. 237–59.

attested elsewhere,[1] does not appear at all in Nehemiah. Possibly it is in the immediate vicinity of the
Tower of the Furnaces (fig. IV), and we may very
well have to identify it with the 'gate of the gardens',
mentioned later by Josephus.[2] The 'gate of the

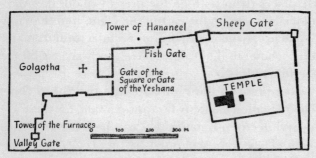

IV. *Gates in the second wall* (ibid., *Plate LXI*)

Yeshana' is less easy to place. What did the name
mean? Are we to understand it as 'gate of the old
city', or 'of the old wall', or simply 'old gate'?[3] It is
possible to defend each of these interpretations, but
in my opinion Fr Vincent has hit upon a better solution. He proposes to make a very slight alteration
in the text—correcting a possible error by a scribe—

[1] II Chron. 26.9; Jer. 31.38; II Kings 14.15.
[2] See above, p. 19.
[3] Revised Version, note 5 to Neh. 3.6. An 'old gate' is mentioned
in Zech. 14.10 (*Translator's note:* Not in A.V. or R.V., but see
Mofatt's translation, and also J. C. H. How's note on this verse in
A New Commentary on Holy Scripture, S.P.C.K., London, 1928, p. 626.)

and to read 'gate of the *Mishneh*',[1] that is to say of the *new district*, the building of which had, as we saw above, necessitated a second wall. Is this gate also the same as the 'gate of Ephraim', in front of which there was a square?[2] This is also Fr Vincent's opinion.[3] He places them both on the present site of the Alexander Hospice, to the east of the Church of the Holy Sepulchre, where important architectural remains have come to light and have been accessible to careful study.[4]

There remain the Fish Gate and the Sheep Gate. Their location can only be approximate, for there are no architectural remains that can be associated with them. They were separated by the Tower of Hananeel,[5] which protected the Temple at the north-west corner of the sacred enclosure, obviously where the Antonia was later to stand. If the Sheep Gate[6] was

[1] *JAT*, I, p. 252. This conjecture finds support in a passage in Zeph. 1.10, where there is mention side by side of *Mishneh* and the Fish Gate.

[2] See Neh. 8.16. (*Translator's note*: 'Street' in A.V. should be 'open space'—cf. R.V., Moffatt, and Knox).

[3] *Ibid.*

[4] Vincent-Abel, *Jérusalem*, II; in particular Plates III–V.

[5] Mentioned several times, apart from Nehemiah: Jer. 31.38; Zech. 14.10. It is also perhaps the 'castle belonging to the Temple' of Neh. 2.8. (Cf. Moffatt's translation.)

[6] The references to it in Neh. (3.1 and 32; 12.39) make it possible to place it not far from the north-east corner of the Temple enclosure. It owed its name to the fact that it was used for bringing in the sheep destined for the sacrifices of Jewish worship. The name was still used in the time of our Lord, as can be seen from John 5.2. (R.V.).

1. *Church of the Holy Sepulchre: South Front*

2. *Church of the Holy Sepulchre: Bell-tower and dome, seen from the Erlöserkirche*

east of the tower, the Fish Gate[1] must have been at some point in the dip of the Tyropoeon, a natural site for a way into the city, as also for a north-south through road.[2]

Is it possible to say through which gate the Good Friday procession passed on its way from Pilate's Praetorium—where Jesus had been condemned—to the place of execution, where He was crucified? Accepting for the moment the authenticity of the traditional site of Golgotha,[3] it is obvious that another question must first be answered: that concerning the location in Jerusalem of the Praetorium of the Roman governor.[4] It was from there that the condemned set out for the place of execution, and from there that we must follow them on that *via dolorosa* which has long since disappeared under tons of débris.

* * *

The traditional route, followed at least once by every modern pilgrim in the course of his visit to the

---

[1] In addition to the passages in Nehemiah, see also II Chron. 33.14; Zeph. 1.10. Doubtless it was here that the men of Tyre sold their fish (Neh. 13.16).

[2] This was later the line of one of the roads of Aelia Capitolina, clearly represented to-day by the street Bab el-Amoud. (See the detailed plan of modern Jerusalem in Vincent, *Jérusalem antique*, Plate III.)

[3] Naturally I shall be returning to this point later.

[4] Vincent, 'Le lithostrotos évangélique', in *RB*, 1952, pp. 513–30; *JAT*, I, pp. 218–21; Benoit, 'Prétoire, Lithostroton et Gabbatha', in *RB*, 1952, pp. 531–50.

Holy Land, starts at the Antonia, the fortress set up by Herod the Great at the north-west corner of the Temple.[1] It is here that some authors place Pilate's residence at the time of the Passion, here that they believe Jesus was tried and sentenced.[2] The so-called *Ecce Homo* basilica is held by others to mark the pre-

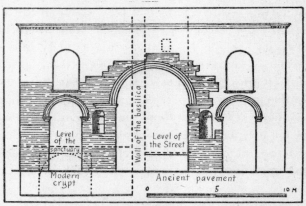

v. *Gate and arch of the Ecce Homo (after Watzinger,* Denkmäler Palästinas, *II, p.* 57)

cise spot where the Roman procurator handed over to the Jews to be crucified 'the Man' who had been brought before him for trial. Actually the arch of the *Ecce Homo* (fig. V) did not exist in the time of our Lord, but belongs quite certainly to a three-bay gateway of the Aelia Capitolina period, and thus

[1] *JAT*, I, pp. 193–216. See also, by the same author, 'L'Antonia, palais primitif d'Hérode', in *RB*, 1954, pp. 87–107.

[2] *JAT*, I, pp. 216–21.

dates from the second century of our era.[1] It cannot therefore, in my opinion, be connected with any of the events of the Passion. On the other hand the magnificent pavement found under the sanctuary, which covers an area of some 1,900 sq. metres, goes back to Herod Agrippa at the latest.[2] On some of the paving-stones are scratched figures used for games (fig. VI), and looking at them one thinks of the sol-

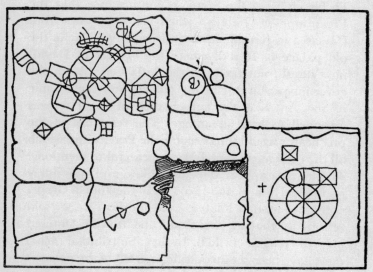

VI. *Roman games scratched on paving-stones (after Vincent and Stève,* JAT, *Plate LIV)*

[1] Vincent-Abel, *op. cit.*, II, pp. 25–30; *JAT*, I, pp. 214, 216. But C. Watzinger, *Denkmäler Palästinas*, II, Leipzig, 1933, p. 57, proposes an earlier date. [2] *JAT*, I, Plate XLIV, pp. 207–8.

diers of the Temple guard whiling away their leisure time moving counters or throwing dice on these roughly drawn squares and circles.[1] Doubtless they were not Pilate's soldiers, but they could have been the soldiers of the 'chief captain' who arrested St Paul (Acts 21.32–4).

There are some seemingly weighty objections to the view that the Antonia was Pilate's residence. Fr Benoit is of the opinion[2] for instance that the Procurator of Judaea, when he came up from Caesarea to Jerusalem, must necessarily lodge in the old palace of Herod, where the 'Tower of David' now stands, not far from the Jaffa Gate. With the governor-procurator in the palace, and the tribune in the Antonia, the surveillance of the city was arranged to best advantage. The residence of the procurator would thus become the Praetorium which all the evangelists save Luke are careful to mention.[3] There Jesus appeared before Pilate and was interrogated by him. But the account in the Fourth Gospel notes the fact that Pilate goes to and fro—we are told repeatedly that he 'went out' and that he 'entered into' the judgement hall. In fact the tribunal ($\beta\hat{\eta}\mu a$) must have been set up outside, in front of the palace.[4] The same Gospel, the soundness of whose historical and geographical sources is now appreciated, alone

[1] For a sketch of these 'games' see *JAT*, I, Plate LIV.
[2] *RB*, 1952, pp. 531–50.
[3] Mark 15.16; Matt. 27.27; John 18.28; 19.9.
[4] For all this see Fr Benoit, in *RB*, 1952, pp. 535, 539–45.

gives certain details: Pilate's judgement seat was in 'a place that is called *Lithostroton*, but in the Hebrew, *Gabbatha*'.[1] Nothing that we know of ancient Jerusalem helps us to identify this site. All we know of it is that it was covered with a pavement[2] and that it must have been on an eminence.[3] In ancient Jerusalem, and in comparison with the Temple, for example, Herod's palace towered massively over the whole of the 'lower town'. All things considered, it is there that I incline to place the Praetorium,[4] and thus from there that I believe the procession left for the place of crucifixion.

Carefully re-reading the different accounts, one is struck by their laconic brevity. It is true that the evangelists have refrained from going into detailed descriptions of the journeys made by Jesus since the previous evening, between the Last Supper and the appearance before Pilate, even though in that case several miles were covered. The Fourth Gospel is the briefest: 'And they took Jesus, and led him away. And he bearing his cross *went forth* into a place called the place of a skull, which is called in the Hebrew Golgotha' (John 19.16–17). Similarly Mark: 'They . . . *led him out* to crucify him' (Mark 15.20). Mark

---

[1] John 19.13. *Gabbatha* is in reality Aramaic.

[2] The term *lithostroton* does not necessarily indicate a mosaic.

[3] The root *gab* signifies 'hump', 'protuberance'.

[4] I therefore support the thesis and arguments of Fr Benoit. Also of this opinion are Fr Abel, *Histoire de la Palestine*, I, p. 425, n. 4; Dalman, *op. cit.*, p. 336; and J. Jeremias, *Golgotha*, Leipzig, 1926, p. 4.

adds the important detail, found also in Matthew and Luke, of the compelling of Simon the Cyrenian, 'who passed by, *coming out of the country*', to carry the cross (Mark 15.21; Matt. 27.32; Luke 23.26).

Did this conscription of Simon take place outside the city? It is not definite, but seems likely. From the Praetorium to the traditional site of Golgotha the distance in a straight line is not great: about a quarter of a mile. Nevertheless we may wonder whether the victims were not made to follow a longer route,[1] through several of the streets of the western part of the city, the custom being to create a greater impression among the population by allowing them to have a closer view of those about to be executed.

It was for this reason too that executions took place in public and in an easily accessible spot. In the present instance the spot thus chosen was called 'the Skull'—in Aramaic, 'Golgotha'. Among Jerusalem place-names it is only mentioned this once, and we have nothing to help us to identify it. Much thought has been given to the interpretation of the name: skulls of those put to death, since it was a place of execution (St Jerome); the skull of Adam,[2] the tomb of the first man having been providentially hidden beneath the knoll on which the cross was set up (Basil

[1] The view of Jeremias, *loc. cit.*, where he quotes several references to this custom, which was Jewish as well as Roman.

[2] For the iconography of this theme, see W. Staude, 'Le crâne-calice au pied de la Croix', in *La Revue des Arts*, 1954, pp. 137–42.

of Caesarea, d. 379).[1] It seems preferable to admit with Fr Vincent[2] merely that the name was given to a rounded rocky hillock—such indeed is the traditional site—because it stood out, just as nowadays in the Near East the name *ras* (head) is still given to certain natural excrescences which have no resemblance whatever to anything human.[3]

Outside the city, Golgotha was near several gates: 80 metres from the Gate of the *Yeshana* (or of Ephraim),[4] 250 metres from the *Gennath* Gate (or Gate of the Gardens). Lacking explicit indications in the Gospel narrative, I do not believe it to be possible to say precisely by what gate Jesus was led out,[5] but what we can say with certainty is that the traditional site agrees strictly with all that we know of the topography of ancient Jerusalem and with the information given in the Gospels.[6]

*   *   *

Tombs and gardens. According to the Fourth Gospel,

[1] Reference given by Jeremias, *op. cit.*, p. 1, n. 6.

[2] Vincent-Abel, *JN*, p. 93.

[3] It would take too long to enumerate all the place-names beginning with *Ras*, of which there are several along the Phoenician coast; Ras en-Naqura, Ras ech-Chaqqa, which the Greeks called *Theou prosopon* (face of god), Ras Shamra, etc.

[4] If it is accepted that two names have been given to the same gate. It will be remembered that *Yeshana* is possibly an error for *Mishneh* (see above, p. 32).

[5] Jeremias, *op. cit.*, p. 6, decides in favour of the *Yeshana*.

[6] John 19.20: '. . . the place where Jesus was crucified was *nigh to the city*.'

'in the place where he was crucified there was a
garden; and in the garden was a new sepulchre,
wherein was never man yet laid' (John 19.41). Is this
information corroborated by what we know of ancient
Jerusalem and by what has been found on the site
of the Church of the Holy Sepulchre? One's first impression, that is to say the impression gained by the
traveller visiting Jerusalem for the first time—is
definitely unfavourable. This is easily explained.
What other reaction is possible to-day, when one
enters a church which seems entirely to have covered
and masked the natural setting, and especially when
it is seen to stand right inside the town, hemmed in
by houses, towers, and minarets, which are themselves enclosed by a magnificent city wall? It is not
hard to understand how in the face of a certain dis-
illusionment, and having regard to ill-founded if not
totally inaccurate knowledge, some pilgrims with the
best of intentions and in all good faith turned with
enthusiasm to the 'Gordon Calvary' and the 'Garden
Tomb'.[1] These at least were unspoilt by religious
buildings, and could be contemplated in a natural
setting that seemed by a miracle to have been preserved through some two thousand years. These
honest devotees of the new shrine were certainly con-
fusing the wall of the Jerusalem where Jesus was put
to death with the wall visible to-day, which can fairly

[1] I shall be dealing with these later. See p. 59.

[40]

be said to be 'modern'.[1] They were unaware that the ramparts of Herod's time, as we have established, did leave the site of the Church of the Holy Sepulchre outside the city; and doubtless no dragoman had pointed out to them, actually *inside* the church (fig. VII), in a corner reserved to the Syrian Jacobites, the remains of an ancient sepulchre with several tombs of the *kôkîm* type,[2] which are purely Jewish in style. Thus it is clear that the Church of the Holy Sepulchre was built on ground that had already in our Lord's day had tombs hewn in it.[3] One cannot insist too strongly on this fact, which is of capital importance for the traditional point of view.

I have already pointed out that the fact that there were also gardens in this sector is implied by the existence of a 'Gate of the Gardens'. This name was not meant to refer so much to carefully cultivated plots in the Western fashion, as to an open space free of habitations,[4] planted here and there with a few trees and agaves, and, being very rocky, having sepulchres hewn in it. One of them was well known. It was that of the high priest John Hyrcanus (d. 104 B.C.), and Josephus mentions it several times in con-

[1] It dates from the time of Suleiman (sixteenth century A.D.).

[2] See the plan and photographs in Vincent-Abel, *JN*, II, pp. 192-3.

[3] These are situated exactly 20 metres west of the edicule of the sepulchre. They are described nowadays as being the Hypogeum of Joseph of Arimathea. There are others a little further to the north.

[4] It is possible of course that isolated houses were built there, but it was more usual in ancient times to shelter the townspeople behind a rampart.

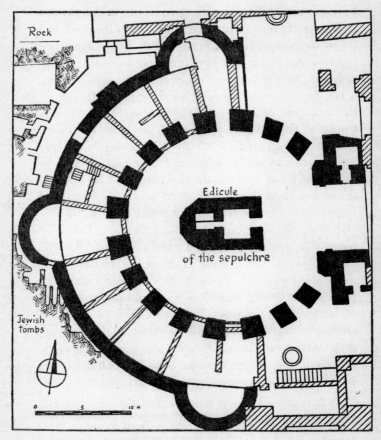

VII. *Jewish tombs in the proximity of the Holy Sepulchre (after Vincent and Abel,* Jérusalem nouvelle, *p. 108)*

nection with the siege of the city as a convenient
landmark. This tomb cannot have been far from the
present Jaffa Gate,[1] in this same area outside the
walls, to the west of Jerusalem.

We know a good deal about the types of tomb that
were in use in the Herodian period. A word or two
about them at this point will help the reader to
understand what the Gospels tell us concerning the
burial of Jesus. Although sometimes the body was
laid in a stone sarcophagus which was itself placed in
a tomb-chamber,[2] it was more generally laid, wrapped
in a winding-sheet, on the bare rock of the tomb.
The latter was only very rarely isolated, usually on
the contrary forming part of a hypogeum which
allowed of a number of burials (fig. VIII). The body
was laid either in a cavity formed by driving a horizontal shaft into the vertical rock face (*kôkîm* type),
or else on a narrow ledge recessed laterally into the
rock which formed a sort of vaulted arch over it
(*arcosolium* type). The simplest tomb arrangement
consisted of an antechamber, which was itself hewn
out of the rock wall (Plates 6 and 7), followed by a
generally square chamber, access to which was gained
through a low doorway, which was closed in a way
I shall discuss later. According to type, the three

[1] *JAT*, p. 91, with references to Josephus.
[2] In Mark 16.6 we find this place designated by the word τόπος.
H. Ingholt, *Parthian Sculptures from Hatra*, connects it with DKT',
found in Palmyra and Hatra, and used to designate a burial-place.

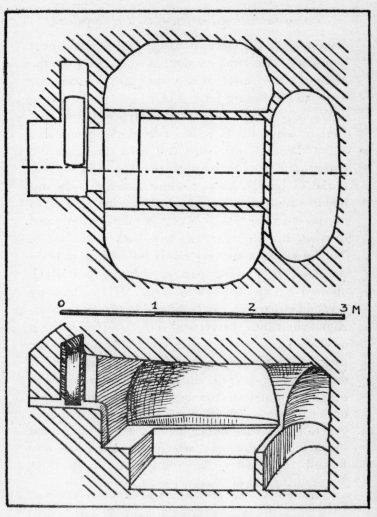

0   1   2   3 M

VIII. *Tomb at Abu-Gosh (after* RB, *1925, p. 277)*

44

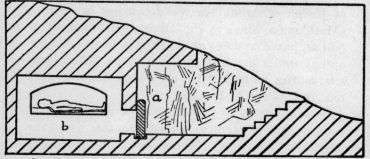

IX. *Our Lord's tomb according to the data in the Gospel narratives*

sides of the chamber[1] were either furnished with three alcoves of the *arcosolium* type, or shafts of the *kôkîm* type, the cavities in each case being a little above ground level, and sometimes being double-banked, an adaptation which considerably increased the number of bodies that could be placed there.[2] This arrangement allowed of variations (one sepulchre might contain both *arcosolia* and *kôkîm*), but was above all capable of considerable extension,[3] in accordance with the size of the families which could thus be kept together after death.

The tomb into which Jesus was carried on the evening of the first Good Friday fits these examples perfectly (fig. IX). Once more we may note how accurate the Gospel records can be. The sepulchre

[1] The fourth was reserved for the entrance.

[2] A particularly fine example is the 'Tomb of the Judges', a photograph of which appears in *JAT*, I, p. 365.

[3] This is the case with the tombs of the 'Kings' and of the 'Judges', the latter having six chambers beyond the vestibule.

of Joseph of Arimathea was hewn out of the rock
(Matt. 27.60; Mark 15.46; Luke 23.53). It must have
had an antechamber cut in the rock face[1] (Plates 6
and 7), into which it was possible to go, *without, however, entering the tomb*. Further, we are expressly told
that one of the first witnesses of the Resurrection,
John, did not go in immediately, and that he had
to *stoop down* in order to see into the interior of the
sepulchre (John 20.5).[2] This detail is also worthy of
note, for the sepulchre doorways are in fact so low[3]
that it is usually necessary to bend down in order to
pass through them. The line of sight of a man who
remained standing outside the aperture would pass
well above it.

This low entrance was generally closed by means
of a stone door[4] having one or two leaves (fig. X),

[1] This is clearly seen in the case of a Jewish tomb on the north
side of Jerusalem, *JAT*, p. 364, fig. 105 (see my Plate 6). In my
reconstruction of the tomb as described in the Gospels (fig. IX), I
part company with Fr Vincent, who postulates a sepulchre consisting
of *two* chambers (*JN*, p. 96, fig. 53). This arrangement is not accepted
by Dalman, *op. cit.*, p. 372, n. 4, with whose view I am in agreement
on this particular detail.

[2] According to John 20.6, Peter went in, which seems to be con-
tradicted by Luke 24.12.

[3] Dalman, *op. cit.*, p. 369, gives the following dimensions: 82×71
cms.; 64×58 cms.; 56×47 cms.; 55×49 cms.; and exceptionally,
1 m. 75 cms. $\times$ 1 m. 13 cms.

[4] There are some very fine examples in the Louvre, originating
either from the Tomb of the Kings (where it was used to close an
inner passage), or from Sur Baher, a village near Bethlehem, or again
from Kefr Yasif near Acre (R. Dussaud, *les monuments palestiniens et
judaïques*, Paris, 1912, pp. 47, 58, 88; André Parrot, *Le Département
des Antiquités orientales*, 2nd ed., 1954, pp. 14–15).

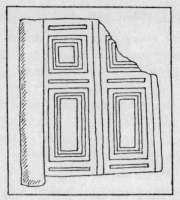

x. *Stone door to an inner chamber in the 'Tombs of the Kings'*
(Louvre, AO 5036)

xi. *Millstone in the 'Tomb of the Herods' (after Vincent, JAT, I,*
Plate LXXXIII)

47

or, more rarely, covered by a flat slab like a millstone (fig. XI). There can be no doubt that this was the stone that was 'rolled', of which the Gospels speak.[1] Of this type we know several excellent examples[2] which show clearly the method of operation, a task requiring at least the strength of one strong man.[3]

The tomb of Jesus was certainly of the *arcosolium* ledge type, for it would not seem possible for anyone to sit in a grave of the *kôkîm* type (Mark 16.5; John 20.12). Doubtless it was on this stone ledge, too, that the napkin and the linen cloths lay that had been used to shroud the body (Luke 24.12; John 20.7). Even without entering the tomb it would be possible to see them from the vestibule (John 20.5),[4] and it was this unaccustomed spectacle, together with the displaced stone, which told the first witnesses that a miraculous event had taken place: Joseph of Arimathea's sepulchre, which had become that of Jesus on the evening of that first Good Friday, was only an empty tomb on Easter Sunday morning!

[1] Matt. 28.2; Mark 15.46; 16.3-4; Luke 24.2.

[2] Dalman, *op. cit.*, p. 370, speaks of 'only three' examples. I myself know four: in the Tomb of the Kings, in the Hypogeum of the Herods, at Abu Gosh (*RB*, 1925, p. 275, Plate XIII), and at Nablus (*RB*, 1910, p. 117). An identical means of closing a doorway is to be seen in a fort in the Hebron district, at Khan ed-Deir (*RB*, 1946, p. 573), and also in the Haris district (*RB*, 1910, p. 117). List in Abel, *RB*, 1925, p. 278.

[3] A point clearly brought out in Mark 16.3, where the women going to the sepulchre on Easter morning said among themselves: 'Who shall roll us away the stone from the door of the tomb?'

[4] Some translations say incorrectly that the winding-sheet was 'on the ground', a detail whose inclusion is not warranted by the Greek text.

3. *Church of the Holy Sepulchre: South doors. On the left lintel: Raising of Lazarus, Entry into Jerusalem, Institution of the Lord's Supper*

II

THE TRADITIONAL SITE

It was in A.D. 326 that the Emperor Constantine ordered the laying of the foundations of a building 'on a scale of rich and imperial costliness', to 'make conspicuous, and an object of veneration to all, the most blessed place of the Saviour's Resurrection'.[1] Three centuries had elapsed since the death of Jesus. This interval of time cannot at first but inspire a certain reserve, for one wonders how the memory of particular sites could have been preserved and handed on during a period in which anything but calm reigned at Jerusalem. To be specific, how was it possible under Constantine to remember still the place where Jesus was crucified and the tomb where He was buried?

To begin with, it is not true to say that the first Christians had absolutely no interest in the places which reminded them of events connected with the life of their Master and Lord. The first link in the chain is that moving reference, made only by the

[1] Eusebius, *Life of Constantine*, III, 25–40. Texts in *Palestine Pilgrims Text Society, Vol. I*; *The Churches of Constantine at Jerusalem*, London, 1897.

evangelist Luke, whom we know to have been scrupulous in the matter of accuracy,[1] in which he tells us that 'the women also, which came with him from Galilee . . . *beheld* the sepulchre, and how his body was laid' (Luke 23.55). Such were the first witnesses.

It is unthinkable that among a people who had always carefully preserved the memory of the tombs of persons of note,[2] an exception should have been made in the case of the crucified Master, particularly since His tomb had been the scene of a prodigious miracle. In Jesus' day and for some time afterwards people could point out the burial-places of Alexander Jannaeus, of John Hyrcanus, and of Helen of Adiabene and her sons.[3] When under Herod Agrippa I the Bezetha district was enclosed within a rampart (the 'third wall'), the result was the addition to the city of an area riddled with tombs, and it is not difficult to imagine that in strict rabbinical eyes this sector must have been considered as unclean.[4] From then on the sepulchre of Jesus was *intra muros*. Hewn

[1] 'Forasmuch as many have taken in hand to draw up a narrative concerning those matters which have been fulfilled among us . . . it seemed good to me also, having traced the course of all things *accurately* from the first, to write. . . .' (Luke 1.1, 3, R.V.).

[2] Patriarchs at Machpelah (Gen. 25.9-10; 50.13), Joseph at Shechem (Josh. 24.32), Joshua at Timnath-Serah (Josh. 24.30), Samson between Zorah and Eshtaol (Judg. 16.31), and so on. The full list would be a very long one.

[3] This is certainly at the 'Tomb of the Kings'. See below, p. 95.

[4] Jeremias, *op. cit.*, p. 9, with texts.

out of the solid rock as it was, it remained unharmed. Also, the district in which it was situated was still called Golgotha, the name being of older origin. There was no reason why the Christians living in Jerusalem should forget its whereabouts, nor had they any motive for refraining from pointing it out to strangers, adherents of the new religion, coming to the Holy City for the first time. Luke the physician, the companion of the apostle Paul, must certainly, after writing as he did, have wished to see with his own eyes what the Galilean women had looked upon on that desolate day of seeming defeat.

At the time of the first Jewish insurrection, in A.D. 66–70, the Christian community fled to Pella,[1] but it returned, in part, once calm had been reestablished. There was no break in continuity until the second revolt (131–4), and there is no reason to suppose that the tomb was destroyed[2] or forgotten.[3]

[1] A town in Peraea, beyond the river Jordan.

[2] One must be wary of accepting without reserve the accounts which tell of the destruction of Jerusalem. We know now what we are to understand by the expression 'a city razed to the ground'! Besides, the Kidron tombs (see below, p. 84), all anterior to A.D. 70, have survived to our own day.

[3] Of that of James the brother of Jesus, killed in A.D. 62, Hegesippus reports that it was still in existence in his day (A.D. 175), on the site of his martyrdom near the Temple. Before the second insurrection the site of the sepulchre of David and Solomon was similarly known. Josephus (*Antiquities*, 16, 7, 1, para. 182) reports that Herod the Great had restored the monument. Its collapse just prior to Bar Kochba's rebellion was considered to be an evil omen for the Jewish people (Dion Cassius, *Historia Romana*, 69.14). For all these points see Jeremias, *op. cit.*, p. 12.

After the suppression of Bar Kochba's movement the political and religious situation in Jerusalem was to undergo radical modification. Jews, Arabs and Samaritans were expelled and strictly forbidden to return. The Christian community, for the most part of Jewish origin and composition, must certainly have been included in the edict, and have had to leave.

Furthermore, Jerusalem was being turned into the Roman city of Aelia Capitolina, with the layout and monuments of a western city. What is more, the Emperor Hadrian seems to have set about a systematic replacement of the old temples and holy places with pagan edifices. The cult of Adonis was established on the site of the Nativity in Bethlehem; at the terebinth of Mamre a market was installed; at the pool of Siloam a nymphaeum was constructed; on the site of the Holy of Holies in the Temple were set up two statues, one of Jupiter and one of the Emperor. Was it merely a chance consequence of the customary town-plan that the Forum of Aelia Capitolina was sited on the Golgotha platform, not far from the 'Square' which was already taking shape in front of the gate of the old wall?[1] The construction of the Forum on this uneven promontory necessitated its levelling, which was done by means of covering it and its tombs with earth. This, while it masked the tombs, also preserved them. The Capitol with its

[1] See above, p. 32.

divinities, Jupiter, Juno and Venus, set the seal on this disruption. It also served, however, to mark the position of what lay buried beneath it.

Besides, even at the time of Aelia Capitolina, Jerusalem was not uninhabited. There existed there a Gentile-Christian community, whose first bishop was one Mark.[1] This was enough to keep the topographical tradition alive, both internally and also externally—for pilgrims began to arrive once more. The earliest recorded pilgrimage is that of Bishop Melito of Sardis, who arrived towards the middle of the second century, and who was the first of many.[2] The number of holy places, genuine or otherwise, soon reached an impressive total, and it is worthy of note that *not once* is mention made of Christian veneration at the sites of Golgotha and the Sepulchre. The explanation of this need not cause any difficulty —they were both hidden under pagan buildings. It is all the more significant that no one dared to pander to the piety of the pilgrims by inventing a spurious Golgotha and Sepulchre in more accessible places, outside Jerusalem, as had been done, for example, in the case of the tombs of David and Solomon and of Adam, which were 'transferred' respectively to Bethlehem and to Hebron.[3] This goes to prove that in

[1] Jeremias, *op. cit.*, p. 19.
[2] Alexander of Cappadocia (*c.* 212), Pionius of Smyrna (d. 250), Firmilian of Caesarea (between 231 and 250). For references to these see Jeremias, *op. cit.*, p. 20, n. 1.
[3] Jeremias, *op. cit.*, pp. 20–1.

this respect the tradition was solid, its authenticity too well recognized for anyone to risk the fabrication —with however good intentions—of an entirely fanciful Golgotha or Sepulchre without any scriptural authority.

It is even more significant that when under Constantine Christianity became the official religion, and was given in Jerusalem complete freedom to enter once more into the possession of its holy places, it was in a sector where every indication seemed against it that Golgotha and the Holy Sepulchre were identified: the site appeared to have been in the midst of the city, and a considerable clearance was now necessary for its original state of hill and rock to be revealed once more. It can only have been that the tradition was compelling: *this* and *no other* was the site.

The earliest testimony we possess on the subject is that of Eusebius, Bishop of Caesarea, who in his *Life of Constantine* (written between 337 and 340) gives what is at first sight a somewhat reticent version of the events:[1]

'After these things [the emperor] beloved of God undertook another memorable work in the province of Palestine. . . . It seemed to him to be a duty to make conspicuous, and an object of veneration to all,

---

[1] *Life of Constantine*, III, 25 ff. English translation in *Palestine Pilgrims Text Society, Vol. I: The Churches of Constantine at Jerusalem,* London, 1897, pp. 1–2. A. N. Grabar, *Martyrium*, Paris, 1946, pp. 234–44, accepts Eusebius' account.

the most blessed place of the Saviour's resurrection
in Jerusalem. And so forthwith he gave orders for
the building of a house of prayer. . . . For ungodly
men (or, rather, the whole race of demons by their
means) set themselves to consign to darkness and
oblivion that divine monument of immortality. . . .
This cave of salvation did certain ungodly and im-
pious persons determine to hide from the eyes of
men. . . . Having expended much labour in bringing
in earth from outside, they cover up the whole place;
and then having raised this to a certain height, and
having paved it with stone, they entirely conceal the
Divine cave beneath a great mound. Next . . . they
prepare above ground a dreadful thing, a veritable
sepulchre of souls, building to the impure demon,
called Aphrodite, a dark shrine of lifeless idols. . . .'

Now the Emperor orders the whole site to be completely cleared and tidied up: 'And as one layer after
another was laid bare, the place which was beneath
the earth appeared; then forthwith, contrary to all
expectation, did the venerable and hallowed monument of our Saviour's resurrection become visible,
and the most holy cave received what was an exact
emblem of His coming to life. . . .' [1] There follows a
description of the shrine which, by imperial command, was then built. [2]

The reader will probably have noticed that Eusebius does not speak of Golgotha, of whose existence

[1] *Loc. cit.*, p. 3.   [2] I shall be describing this later.

and location, however, he is aware.[1] This omission
is doubtless to be explained by the fact that what
principally interests the biographer is the restoration
to view of the Sepulchre, everything else being left
in the background.[2] However, in A.D. 333 the Pilgrim
of Bordeaux, visiting Jerusalem, refers explicitly to
the 'little hill of Golgotha where the Lord was
crucified, and within a stone's throw, the crypt where
His body was laid and where on the third day He
rose again.'[3]

Thus the Constantinian building, which was in
course of construction at the time, must still have
permitted the visitor to see the essential configuration
of the ground, which was as time passed to be more
and more effectively masked. One can well understand how less than a score of years later, by A.D. 350,
Cyril of Jerusalem found it necessary to embark on a
lengthy explanation.[4] But for that very reason his
testimony is the more interesting, for he shows us
how foreigners and the uninitiated were already find-
ing themselves able to formulate objections on the
ground that the site was 'in the middle of the town'.
By the fourth century people had only the vaguest
notion of what Jerusalem was like in Jesus' day. In-

[1] 'Golgotha: the place of the skull, where Jesus was crucified; it
is to be seen at Aelia, north of the hill of Sion,' *Onomasticon*, 74. 19–21.
Written about the year 335.

[2] Dalman, *op. cit.*, pp. 349, 354; Jeremias, *op. cit.*, p. 19.

[3] Geyer, *Itinera Hierosolymitana saeculi iiii–viii*, 1898, 20–3. It is
actually 44 yds. from the Calvary to the Holy Sepulchre.

[4] Cyril of Jerusalem, *Catecheses*.

deed, Cyril in his defence of the traditional site was reduced to using the Song of Songs as a support for his argument. The site received too a whole appendage of miraculous legend which we shall not attempt to justify either archaeologically or historically, but which provides an example of the progression in terms of the marvellous which is characteristic of the evolution and development of legends. In this case we have the cycle of the Invention of the Cross, to which the name of Helena, the mother of Constantine, has become attached.[1] For not only has Golgotha been rediscovered, but the very crosses too, upon which Jesus and, as the Gospels relate, His two companions were put to death. But how was Jesus' cross to be identified and distinguished from the other two? The problem was solved, however; a woman mortally sick was immediately restored to health on being brought into contact with the true cross. This miracle was surpassed by another: a dead man revived when he was laid upon the wood of the cross.

These legendary additions[2] are like a froth which we must not allow to hide the historicity of the events and their supporting evidence. It is the lot of tradition constantly to become weighed down with such addi-

[1] This progression in the marvellous has been carefully studied by Jeremias, *op. cit.*, pp. 30–3, where he gives references to the authors concerned. The legend evolved between the years 395 and 400. See also Vincent-Abel, *op. cit.*, II, pp. 191, 202–3.

[2] There are plenty more: the discovery of the superscription, and of the nails used in the crucifixion. As for the wood of the true cross, according to Cyril 'the whole world is filled with its fragments'!

tions. What we must do is to remove all this useless accumulation and rediscover the truth that lies hidden beneath. Critical study of the whole of the literary evidence, carried out independently by specialists as different in outlook and as competent as Fr Vincent, G. H. Dalman, and J. Jeremias, has in fact convinced them all that tradition does not err in locating Golgotha and the tomb of Jesus in the present Church of the Holy Sepulchre. Since archaeology not only does not deny the accuracy of the tradition, but on the contrary reinforces it at every point, I do not see what further objection there could be. I shall not however go so far as to say that the matter is closed, and that it is *absolutely certain* that the Sepulchre of Jesus lies beneath the edicule in the Church of the Holy Sepulchre. However, what I do believe to be established is that the overwhelming probability is that it is there and nowhere else, in this Jerusalem which has undergone such radical changes since Pilate's day. The element of uncertainty remaining is minute—and it does not seem possible to eliminate it. On the other hand, we must eliminate without the slightest hesitation the 'Gordon Calvary' and the 'Garden Tomb' associated with it. Many people having been misled by this mirage, it is not out of place to say here as emphatically as possible that the evidence that has been forged from time to time in the attempt to authenticate this new holy place rests only on shifting sand, and that archaeology lends it no support whatever. On the contrary, archaeology condemns it out of hand.

*   *   *

Gordon Calvary and Garden Tomb. [1] In 1867, a resident in Jerusalem who owned some land in the immediate neighbourhood of a cave known as 'Jeremiah's Grotto', had in the course of an excavation come upon the entrance to a sort of cavern full of bones, with a cross painted in red visible on one of its walls. The man took the trouble to seek further information on his find from one of the archaeological authorities of Jerusalem at that time, the architect Schick. The latter saw in it nothing more than a quite ordinary tomb. Shortly afterwards the entire contents were removed. No written evidence was found, and Schick considered it of such minor interest that he did not even think it necessary to write an account of it. These points are important enough to be insisted upon in the light of what was to follow. The owner of the land, however, died shortly afterwards, and for some time no one gave any further thought to this insignificant discovery.

In 1883 General Gordon, who two years later was to make his name famous through his heroic defence of Khartoum, had just arrived in Jerusalem. Like many others, he was an amateur student of biblical questions, and he believed he could see in the topo-

[1] L. H. Vincent, 'Garden Tomb', in *RB*, 1925, pp. 401–31.

graphy of the Holy City the actual image of the
stages of Revelation. He had been struck by the
appearance of the hill which lies on the north side
of Jerusalem, about 150 metres from the present wall,
and which bears the name of Ez-zahira.[1] Its surface
marked by quarries and the visible traces of grottoes,
it presented to the observer a certain resemblance to
the features of a death's head. It was not, however,
this aspect which had struck the general,[2] but the
fact that if one pictured ancient Jerusalem as a
skeleton[3] lying on its side, with its feet at the Pool of
Siloam, its seat at the Dome of the Rock, i.e. the
Temple, its head would actually lie on one of the
hills of the Bezetha, outside the walls. Nothing more
was needed to convince the general that this must
be the site of Calvary (fig. XII), and he expressed
the belief that the actual tomb of Jesus and the Emperor Constantine's commemorative church would
be found in the immediate vicinity. As to the view
he took of the grave uncovered at the foot of the
western face of his Calvary, the evidence is conflict-
ing. According to Schick, Gordon considered it to be
that of Christ, whereas his close friend Wilson de-
clares that 'General Gordon visited this tomb but

[1] Dalman, *op. cit.*, p. 348.
[2] Later on, other pilgrims were more sensible of this point—in
particular a number of my fellow Protestants, not well enough versed
in the problems of New Testament archaeology.
[3] Sir C. W. Wilson, *Golgotha and the Holy Sepulchre*, Palestine Exploration Fund, London , 1906, p. 201, fig. 12.

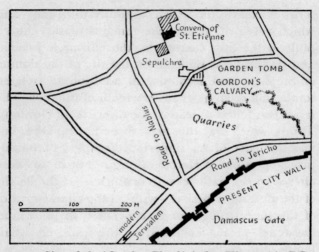

XII. *Site of the 'Garden Tomb' (after Vincent, in* RB,
1925, p. 402)

makes no direct reference to it.'[1] For all those who
already opposed or were to go on opposing the traditional view,[2] only Schick's assertion was to be
believed. From then on *Gordon's Tomb* was associated
with *Gordon's Calvary.*

In 1883, the same year as that in which Gordon
came to Jerusalem,[3] the Dominicans, who had bought
some land in the same district, were setting about a

[1] Schick, in *Quarterly Statement*, 1892, p. 122; Wilson, *op. cit.*, p.
199, n. 4.

[2] Among the first was the German Pastor Otto Thenius, who
sought Calvary on the same hill as early as 1842. (Dalman, *op. cit.*,
p. 348).

[3] Lagrange, *Saint Etienne et son sanctuaire à Jérusalem*, p. 106.

series of excavations which continued until 1893, and which revealed, firstly, the remains of the church built in the fifth century by the patriarch Juvenal and the Empress Eudoxia on the site of the stoning of Stephen, and secondly, in addition to isolated tombs, a large hypogeum hewn out of the rock. The latter was found to lead in the direction of Gordon's Tomb, which was thus seen to be not isolated, but forming part of an important complex of burial-places, possibly of Herodian origin, but in any case altered in the sixth-seventh centuries—at the height of the Byzantine period—with all the characteristics of the time: trough-tombs covered with horizontal flagstones, crosses engraved on the walls, Christian lamps, and epitaphs.

Four inscriptions had been found. One, in the hypogeum, was worded as follows: 'Tomb of the deacon Euthymios Pindiris'. Another, from a vault situated to the north of the Eudocian basilica, read as follows: 'Tomb of the deacon Nonnus Onesimus, of the holy Anastasis of Christ and of this monastery.'[1]

There could be no doubt of the interpretation. This was the sepulchre of a cleric who as well as being a member of a monastic community was *also* an official of the Church of the Resurrection, that is of the Holy Sepulchre.[2] The only possible explana-

[1] Facsimile in Vincent, *loc. cit.*, p. 409.
[2] This was no more surprising than the discovery on the Mount of Olives and in Gethsemane of the tombs of a deacon and two

[62]

tion of the sensation caused by the discovery of this inscription is that some were misled through lack of knowledge of epigraphy, while others had ulterior motives, the strongest of which was the need to furnish a documentary basis for the new holy place. From then on there took place an obvious falsification of the evidence, in a series of signed and unsigned articles, the most serious misrepresentation being the assertion that in one of the inscriptions the deceased was said to be 'buried near his Lord'.[1] No one has ever been able to produce either a photograph or a copy of this suggestive text—and the reason is that it never existed. Nevertheless the whole structure was erected on the basis of it. It furnished the guarantee which turned well-intentioned pilgrims into advocates of this shaky claim. For a short time the Anglican clergy supported it, and the land in which Gordon's Tomb was situated was purchased. The name became changed to Garden Tomb; but it is only fair to remark that after this burst of enthusiasm the representatives in Jerusalem of the Church of England had second thoughts, and withdrew energetically and finally from the impossible position to which their inexperience had led them, hedged about as it was with fraud and misrepresentation. The

janitors of the same Anastasis. No one, however, has, nor ever would have thought of looking for the Holy Sepulchre on the Mount of Olives or in Gethsemane! Texts and references in Vincent, *loc. cit.*, p. 409, n. 1.

[1] Vincent, *loc. cit.*, pp. 410, 418, 422–3.

Garden Tomb ceased to be a Holy Place, and was thereafter no more than a curiosity.[1]

Meanwhile, expert archaeological opinion had been forthcoming, and rarely can it have been so unanimous.[2] As I mentioned above, the Garden Tomb forms part of a funerary complex which, if it dates from the Herodian period—which has still to be proved—has retained absolutely nothing of its original appearance. The trough-graves, the crosses painted on the walls and cantoned with the letters A and Ω, are undoubtedly Byzantine (fifth and sixth centuries). Furthermore, there are traces (conduits, feeding-troughs, bolt-slots)[3] of mediaeval use as an abode of the living rather than the dead. The wheel was to come full circle: the place once more became a charnel-house, and it was this which came to light in 1867. No one at that time could have guessed at the exalted destiny that was in store for this 'insignificant' burial-place. I have dealt with it here simply

[1] On the iron gate of the enclosure the following notice may be read: 'The Garden Tomb. Believed by many to be where the body of our Lord lay. I am the Resurrection and the Life.' Underneath, more discreetly in smaller though no less legible characters, one reads: 'All visitors are requested to contribute 5 piastres (about 10s.) to the maintenance fund.'

[2] I quote here only the most authoritative verdicts: 'Nothing whatever can be said in favour of the tomb'(Macalister, *QS*, 1907, p. 232); 'Why should we do the daydreams of Gordon and Conder the honour of taking them seriously?' (Clermont-Ganneau, *RAO*, VIII, p. 24); '[Garden Tomb] is one of the most insignificant in the great necropolis' (Wilson, *op. cit.*, p. 117); 'The rocky grave . . . cannot seriously be considered as Jewish' (Dalman, *op. cit.*, p. 348, n. 5).

[3] Vincent, *loc. cit.*, p. 419.

because it was necessary to say again, in the most categorical terms, that nothing was ever more certain than that the Garden Tomb is a myth. One hopes that no sensible person will ever again be misled by it.[1]

[1] It is worth while recalling what the late Jean Laroche wrote twenty years ago about a pamphlet which had just been published under the title *Le Calvaire et la tombe du Christ*, once more defending Gordon's theory: 'Its text is most unreliable, and calculated to cause the liveliest of reactions among those who, after having accepted its claims as well-founded, find on further study how unsatisfactory they are' (*Journal des Ecoles du Dimanche*, April, 1935). I have refrained from quoting names out of consideration for honoured and respected men whose good faith and sincerity had been abused.

III

THE CHURCH OF THE HOLY SEPULCHRE

While it seems that in all likelihood the traditional site of Golgotha and the tomb of Jesus are to be considered as authentic, it must be added at once that very little of it is visible to-day under the building which covers and masks it. It is easy to understand the astonishment and even perplexity of pilgrims who expect to see 'something', and who are shown only an old church, whose very shape is not at first evident,[1] and which has not preserved the simplicity and majesty of that at Bethlehem, for example. How amidst all this profusion of altars, chapels, pillars, gilt, lamps and icons is one to recognize the hill of the Skull and Joseph of Arimathea's new tomb? How can we trace here the events of the first Good Friday and the victory of Easter? My intention is not to list all the disappointments and disillusionments that await the inquirer, but to help him to see how and

---

[1] 'The first sensation one has on coming into this building is an oppressive feeling of being in a labyrinth, a sensation of chaos' (Vincent, in *Jérusalem*, II, p. 105).

by what architectural stages the natural topography of the site has come to be so hidden.

The building as it now stands is the composite work of several periods, in which the following successive stages are recognizable: the original Constantinian building (fourth century); two restorations —that of the patriarch Modestos (seventh century), after the burning down of the church by the Persians in 614, and that of Constantine Monomachos (eleventh century) who attempted to repair the depredations of the caliph Hakim (1009); lastly the extensive work carried out by the Crusaders, who devoted half a century (1099–1149) to the restoration of the dilapidated structures to the dignity, if not the splendour, that was theirs in the time of Constantine. Leaving out of account all the alterations, repairs and consolidations that have been carried out, and confining ourselves to the decisive phases, we can briefly say that the Church of the Holy Sepulchre bore and still bears double witness to a *Byzantine* foundation and a *Romanesque* tradition. While the second is visible at once in both structure and ornament, the first is much less obvious, and close study is necessary if it is to be recognized with certainty and its character appreciated. [1]

[1] In all that follows I make reference to the undisputed authority of Fr Vincent, who has analysed the building stone by stone, and is always careful to distinguish between fact and hypothesis. His work is unlikely to be superseded for some time to come. Anything written by others now could only be a recapitulation.

Entering by the double Romanesque doorway (Plate I),[1] its lintels carved with scenes from the last week of the life of Jesus,[2] the visitor bears to the left to find himself beneath a rotunda (fig. XIII, A),

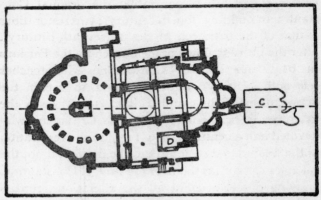

XIII. *Church of the Holy Sepulchre*

against which, to the east, stands a church (B) which has no nave, but only a transept, and a choir and ambulatory with chapels radiating from its eastern end.[3] On examination it is seen that there are represented two architectural periods, separated by a considerable lapse of time and corresponding to two

---

[1] The right-hand door is now walled up.

[2] On the north door, from left to right: the raising of Lazarus, the entry into Jerusalem, and the Last Supper.

On the south door: intertwined foliage among which are figures of men, birds, and fantastic creatures. Reproductions in Vincent, *Jérusalem*, II, Plate XXIX. See my Plate III.

[3] A detailed plan is to be found in Vincent, *op. cit.*, Plate XIII.

quite different conceptions. The rotunda is in fact Constantinian, while the church dates from the time of the Crusaders. The latter, instead of setting about the reconstruction of the earlier buildings, proceeded to rebuild completely, and it is this new departure which inevitably produces the incongruity of which even the least knowledgeable observer is conscious.

Constantine's architects had had different aims, and the plans they put into effect were proof of their audacity as well as their sense of harmony. What was it that they, and the emperor whose wishes they must certainly have been carrying out, had in mind? Our most ancient literary source is once more to be found in Eusebius, Bishop of Caesarea,[1] though it is a pity that his bias detracts from the precision of a description which we could frequently have liked to see more detailed and illustrated by figures. However, if one applies reasoned criticism[2] to the text, one can extract from among the floods of panegyric and adulation certain indications whose importance it is impossible to underestimate, and which permit one to form some idea of the completed building even before one has had any recourse to archaeology. Along a west-east longitudinal axis four elements were, it seems, juxtaposed: a rotunda, a church, and two courtyards surrounded by covered porticoes and

[1] *Op. cit.*
[2] See that of Fr Vincent, *op. cit.*, pp. 155–64.

forming an enclosure around the church (fig. XIV).[1]

It is clear that Eusebius is mainly concerned to emphasize the importance of the 'divine cave', i.e.

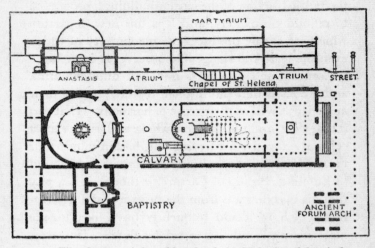

xiv. *The Constantinian Church of the Holy Sepulchre (after Vincent and Abel,* op. cit., *Plate XXXIII)*

the tomb, but from what he writes it is impossible to know *how* 'round about the cave of salvation' the sanctuary was raised 'on a scale of rich and imperial

[1] See the diagram of the building reconstructed in accordance with Eusebius' description, in Vincent, *op. cit.*, p. 155, fig. 102. A. Grabar, *Martyrium*, p. 252, considers that the basis of the *martyrium* in Jerusalem is to be found in the *heroa*, with their theme of two religious buildings (a basilica and a tomb) within a single enclosure, one of them being chiefly a memorial, and the other a hall destined for large gatherings of worshippers.

costliness'. However, all the architects and archaeologists agree that the rock in which Joseph of
Arimathea's sepulchre was hewn was largely cut
away so as to isolate the tomb.[1] It became an edicule
(fig. VII), 'the chief part of the whole', which 'the
liberality of the emperor beautified with choice
columns and with much ornament'; it was then
made the centre of a domed rotunda[2] (Plate 2). It
was later called the *Anastasis* (Resurrection).

The second part of the complex received the name
of *Martyrium*. It was a basilica with a nave and four
aisles,[3] terminated by a single apse. The entrance
was not at the west end (which faced the Anastasis),
but to the east, towards the ancient *cardo maximus* of
the colony of Aelia. It was in fact with reference to
this ancient colonnaded road that the whole architectural group was planned. The façade of the
temenos wall was pierced by a triple gateway,[4] which

[1] This is indicated also by Cyril of Jerusalem: 'The protection of
the rock . . . has now disappeared, for the vestibule was levelled so
that the present building might be better ordered.'

[2] With a radius of 60 ft. (Vincent, *op. cit.*, p. 171, fig. 107). According to Grabar, *op. cit.*, p. 279, the plan of the edicule was square.
This latter author assigns to Constantine several architectural features which were thought to be of later date than the Persian
invasion of 614. This does not accord with the views of Vincent and
Abel.

[3] Length: 148 ft., according to Vincent, *op. cit.*, p. 172. It is
important to note, with Vincent, that of the *Martyrium* 'no vestige
remains visible'.

[4] Two of the bays are still visible to-day in the Alexander Hospice
and the Coptic convent. For an elevation of this façade see Vincent,
op. cit., Plate VI.

was approached by a formal flight of steps. Passing through this doorway, one found oneself in an atrium surrounded by an arcaded walk. The visitor would cross this to find himself at the triple doorway to the basilica, which had been built not, as one might logically expect, with reference to Golgotha,[1] but instead to cover a crypt (the 'chapel of St Helena' and the cave of the Invention of the Cross), which was actually a subterranean church with a nave and two aisles and a central dome.[2] In this it was like the Constantinian basilica at Bethlehem, which also stood over a grotto—that of the Nativity.

From the Martyrium, however, the faithful must have been able to proceed both to the Calvary and to the Anastasis. The former was certainly isolated, as can be seen from the account given by Sylvia Ætheria, who made a pilgrimage to Jerusalem about the year 395. She clearly distinguishes three parts: Anastasis, Martyrium, and *ad Crucem* (Calvary). It has been possible to calculate that the level of the Martyrium was from 4 metres to 4 metres 50 below

---

[1] Eusebius, as I have already pointed out, makes no mention whatever of Golgotha. Grabar, *op. cit.*, p. 253, expresses the opinion that the presence of Golgotha in this place 'must have determined the Constantinian builders to give it an architectural expression which would distinguish it from the buildings over the Holy Sepulchre itself and the basilica, which was intended at first for the *synaxis*, but was soon to become in addition the guardian of the sacred grotto of the Invention of the Cross.'

[2] For a plan, section, and elevation see Vincent, *op. cit.*, pp. 132–4, figs. 84–7.

that of the Calvary.[1] The visitor therefore 'climbed up' to the latter, and Fr Vincent considers that the ascent could be made by one of two staircases, one of which led from the end of one of the southern aisles of the basilica, and the other from the inner atrium,[2] which was situated between the apse of the basilica and the door of the Anastasis rotunda.

There is one invaluable document which gives us a diagrammatic reproduction of the Constantinian construction. This is the 'Madeba map', a magnificent mosaic found in Transjordan in 1884 and studied in 1887. It dates from the sixth century.[3] Among other things it gives a plan on which the Church of the Holy Sepulchre is reproduced.[4] Despite the simplified nature of the diagram (fig. XV), the steps leading up to the church are clearly recognizable,

[1] Vincent, *op. cit.*, p. 173; cf. also p. 100: 'The pavement of the Calvary is at an average level of 4 m. 50 above that of the rotunda.'

[2] Describing this atrium, Eusebius praises its floor which 'a polished stone pavement adorned, bounded by long porticoes which ran round continuously on three sides' (*Life of Constantine*, III, 35). Direct access to it could be gained from outside by means of a doorway called the door 'of the atrium of the Holy Cross'.

[3] The most recent comprehensive study of the Madeba map is that by R. T. O'Callaghan (d. 1954) in *Dictionnaire de la Bible*, *Supplément*, Part XXVI, under *Madaba (carte de)*, col. 637–703, with a bibliography.

[4] Vincent-Abel, *op. cit.*, pp. 179–80, Plates XXXI–XXXII. Grabar, *op. cit.*, p. 236, considers that the artist of the mosaic of Madeba clearly wished to indicate that the founder of the city had his *heròon* in the heart of Jerusalem. According to the same author (p. 256) it was the *tomb of Christ* which in the original architectural scheme was the true *martyrium* (i.e. the commemorative monument of a holy place), although it was not specifically designated by this name.

xv. *The Church of the Holy Sepulchre in the Madeba mosaic*
(ibid., *Plate XXXII*)

together with the triple doorway in the façade of the outer atrium, the tympanum of the façade and the roof of the Martyrium, and lastly the hemispherical dome covering the rotunda of the Anastasis.[1]

, Even though the artist who made the mosaic has combined two façades in one, by omitting from his view the exterior atrium, one could hardly wish for better confirmation of the suggested reconstruction of Constantine's work. After making 'conspicuous, and an object of veneration to all, the most blessed place of the Saviour's resurrection', the emperor had added to it a 'house of prayer'. However, the appearance of the site had undergone a profound alteration. The sepulchre had been isolated from the surrounding rock, the antechamber obliterated, and the rock ornamented, we are told, 'with lustrous adornment'. Golgotha too had been excavated, leaving, however, a 'projection of undressed rock'[2] on which a memorial cross had been set up. Such was the condition of the natural objects presented to the veneration of the faithful, whose imaginations, however, were arrested even more by the buildings and relics.[3] To see and

[1] To the Madeba mosaic must be added an ivory in the Bibliothèque Nationale in Paris (illustrated in Vincent-Abel, *op. cit.*, p. 182, fig. 110), which in spite of differences of detail clearly shows the Martyrium and the Anastasis.   [2] Vincent-Abel, *op. cit.*, p. 188.

[3] The precision of these was already quite beyond all imagination: they included Solomon's ring, the horn of the anointing of David, the charger on which John the Baptist's head was placed, the onyx chalice from the Last Supper, the reed, sponge, superscription, and nails used in the Crucifixion, together with fragments of the true Cross, etc.

kneel in prayer at the tomb of Christ was thereafter
to be the chief motive of that great wave of pilgrim-
ages of which the Pilgrim of Bordeaux was the herald
(A.D. 333) and which has never stopped since.

*   *   *

I said above that the Constantinian building was
burned down in 614 by the Persians, who had succeeded in taking Jerusalem in the course of the ebb
and flow of the long struggle between the Byzantines
and Sassanids which had been going on ever since
Roman times. Restoration work was carried out by
Modestos, the *higoumenos* of the Convent of St Theo-
dosius. His efforts were concentrated on the Anastasis,
for it was the safeguarding of the Sepulchre for which
most concern was felt. It naturally remained isolated,
and according to the pilgrim Arculf (in Jerusalem
about A.D. 670), on the right of the visitor entering
the cavern was the funerary ledge, hewn out of the
rock and overhung by an *arcosolium* vault from which
were suspended eight lamps burning day and night. [1]
The stone which had served to close the entrance to
the tomb was no longer in one piece, having no doubt
been broken by the Persians. Its pieces were later
used as altar-slabs.

The inner atrium had become the 'Holy Garden'.
The Calvary, covered by a church, itself contained

[1] Vincent-Abel, *op. cit.*, p. 221, gives full details of the interior
and exterior appearance of the edicule.

another, which had for certain oriental pilgrims
become the 'church and tomb of Adam',[1] while at
the foot of the mount of Golgotha the sacrifice of
Isaac was commemorated, with the wooden table on
which Abraham had been about to offer up his son!
Finally, a noble staircase led down from the Martyrium into the crypt 'where the venerable Queen
Helena found the Holy Rood'.

In 1009, however, disaster again overtook the
sacred buildings. Jerusalem had been in Musulman
hands since 638, and had frequently suffered scenes
of violence. But none of them equalled that to which
the Caliph Hakim attached his name. In obedience
to his command, the Church of the Holy Sepulchre
was demolished. Its end, however, had not yet come.
Hakim's successors showed more tolerance, and came
to terms with the Byzantines. Shortly after the acces-
sion of Constantine Monomachos (1042) the Church
of the Resurrection was restored (1048). The Martyrium was not rebuilt, attention being confined once
more to the tomb itself. The Anastasis had suffered
severely from the picks of the demolishers in 1009,
and very little can have remained of the tomb and
even of the surrounding rock.[2] It was therefore
necessary to reconstruct the cave 'in masonry' on the
original site, the whole being covered with a 'strong
construction'. The last trace of the natural state of
the site was obliterated. On Golgotha, however,

[1] *Ibid.*, p. 229. [2] *Ibid.*, p. 253.

[77]

which was still crowned with an oratory decorated with mosaics, the summit of the rock was still bare where it emerged from a marble-flagged pavement.[1] On the 15th July 1099 it was the turn of the Crusaders to enter Jerusalem. That same evening they went up to the Church of the Holy Sepulchre. 'They washed their hands and their feet, took off their blood-stained garments and donned new robes, and then went barefoot into the Holy Places.'[2] 'The native Christians, who had come out in procession to meet them, conducted them to the Church of the Holy Sepulchre to the accompaniment of hymns and acts of thanksgiving. There every man fell with his face to the ground, his arms making the sign of the Cross.' 'Each seemed still to see before him the crucified body of Jesus Christ.'[3]

*   *   *

The Crusaders had two clear courses of action from which to choose: either to rebuild the whole Constantinian complex, now almost totally ruined, or simply to confine themselves to the more modest building of Constantine Monomachos. They chose a middle-of-the-way solution which consisted in limiting their efforts but nevertheless bringing within one edifice the essential sites of the Passion, namely, the tomb and Golgotha, while allowing for direct access

[1] *Ibid.*, p. 254.
[2] René Grousset, *L'épopée des Croisades*, Paris, 1939, p. 45.
[3] *Ibid.*, p. 46.

to the subterranean church dedicated to the memory of Helena and the Invention of the Cross. In the words of William of Tyre they included 'in one and the same building' 'quite small oratories' until then *outside* the Church of the Resurrection. Even on this reduced scale the project was an ambitious one, and it took exactly half a century to execute it. It was in fact on the 15th July 1149 that it was possible at last to celebrate the conclusion of the undertaking.[1]

Completely restored, the circular edicule was preceded by a rectangular vestibule, in which had been set up an altar containing a fragment believed to be from the stone that closed the sepulchre. The 'tomb' was still the little rectangular chamber with the funerary ledge on the right, though there cannot have been much of the original rock remaining.

The romanesque church was built against the rotunda, and was no more than a choir, a transept, an ambulatory and an apse with three chapels radiating from it. The axis of the building, instead of coinciding with that of the edicule, was deflected noticeably towards the north, and thus part of the church was outside the area of the Constantinian inner atrium. Above the crossing was a dome,[2] and

[1] This date is given by Vincent-Abel, *op. cit.*, p. 280, from which I have taken the information which follows. See the recent account in E. Lambert, 'L'architecture des Templiers', in *Bulletin monumental,* CXII, 1954, pp. 7–60, and the summary by R. Dussaud, in *Syria,* XXXI, 1954.

[2] It can be seen in Plate 2 to the right of the darker-coloured dome of the rotunda.

at floor level the *omphalos* of the ground was still shown. As for the Little Mount of Calvary, it could be climbed by several staircases, one from the fore-court of the church and another from the south ambulatory. The chapel covering it was dressed entirely with marble, but the bare hump of rock on which the Cross was set up was still left open to view. This chapel, with its mosaics, was now a part of the main building, though on a higher level. [1] The chapel of St Helena, on the other hand (fig. XVI), was on a considerably lower level. [2] One went down into it by means of a staircase of some thirty steps, which opened from the south of the centre chapel of the three radiating from the apse of the church. Four columns, surmounted by dissimilar Byzantine capi-tals, supported the domed roof of the crypt (Plate 5). Of the whole of the Church of the Holy Sepulchre as it is to-day, this is by far the most impressive part. Away from the flood of tourists, dimly lit, nothing else in this heterogeneous church is more conducive to meditation.

In putting the main entrance to their basilica on the south side, the Crusaders were following the precedent set by the Constantinian builders (fig. XIV), who had constructed at that point an entrance to the inner atrium, so as to give immediate access to the Anastasis. The position of their building meant

[1] 4 m. 50 above the pavement of the rotunda.
[2] 5 m. 60 below the same pavement.

5. *Church of the Holy Sepulchre: Chapel of St Helena*

6. *Jewish tomb of the Herodian period, showing antechamber hewn out the rock*

7. *Jewish tomb with decorated façade*

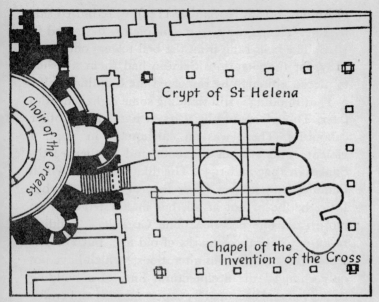

XVI. *The crypt of St Helena in the Church of the Holy Sepulchre*
(ibid., *p. 271*)

that the Franks did not intend to rebuild the Martyrium, so that provision for access on the south side was practically unavoidable. The pilgrims would thus enter the sacred precinct by a double doorway, and leaving Golgotha on the right were at once in sight of the rotunda. At the foot of the Little Mount of Calvary several Frankish kings were laid to rest: Godfrey of Bouillon (d. 18th July, 1100), Baldwin I (d. 1118), Baldwin II (d. 21st August, 1131), Fulke of Anjou (d. 15th November 1144), were buried side by side. Their graves were completely destroyed in 1810. The bells rang from the bell-tower[1] only until 1187, for the victorious Saladin had them smashed to pieces, although he respected the building itself.

That building is still standing some eight centuries later. Though spared by wars, it has suffered other calamities. There was an earthquake in 1545, a violent conflagration in 1808, and further earthquakes in 1927 and 1937. The dilapidation to which buildings are subject when they are cared for but little, badly, or not at all, has manifested itself on more than one occasion. The Crusaders' building bears not only these marks of old age, but also the scars left by outrageous alterations,[2] which have not only changed the architectural lines of a building conceived and executed by expert masters and craftsmen, but also completed the destruction of what little remained of the rocky hill of the time of Constantine, if not of Gospel times. In 1809 the edicule of the tomb, where already so little had survived all the vicissitudes to which I have referred, was razed, this time to the rock. The least said the better about the frightful kiosk which now stands in the centre of the

[1] A bell-tower is first mentioned in 1154, by the Arab Idrisi (Vincent-Abel, *op. cit.*, p. 285).

[2] That for example of 1810, with which is associated the name of one Comninos the Caulker, a Greek from Mytilene.

rotunda (Plate 4), where rival confessions [1] are daily ready to come to blows in order to be the sole worshippers there. At certain times of day, and on certain feasts, amid the distressing tumult and din of the processions, one would very readily agree with those words spoken on Easter morning (Luke 24.5): 'Why seek ye the living among the dead? He is not here. . . .'

[1] In the eighteenth century the allocation was as follows (I quote only the main divisions): the Greeks had the choir of the Crusaders' church, the north half of the Little Mount of Calvary, and the Chapel of Adam; the Latins possessed the edicule of the tomb, the south side of the Calvary, and the site of the Invention of the Cross; the Armenians controlled the Chapel of St Helena; the Copts had the right of officiating at the rear of the edicule of the tomb; the Syrians worshipped in a chapel near the so-called Hypogeum of Joseph of Arimathea; in our own day, if I remember correctly, the Abyssinians had to be content with the roof-terraces. Each confession is obsessed with the idea of maintaining the *status quo*, and every departure from the time-table of services in the few zones left undivided at once establishes a precedent which is thereupon considered as having the force of law.

IV

TOMBS AND BURIALS IN
ANCIENT JERUSALEM

Joseph of Arimathea's sepulchre, in which the body
of Jesus was placed on Good Friday evening, no
longer exists; and the tombs which I referred to as
being inside the Church of the Holy Sepulchre give
us to-day only a very imperfect idea of the large vaults
and the burial customs of our Lord's time. It will
therefore be useful to say a few words now about
some of the mausoleums that are still visible, and
which lack only the bodies once laid to rest there.
I shall confine myself here to those which, rightly or
wrongly, traditionally have biblical associations.

Among the thousands of tombs (Plate 8), some
very ancient, some less so, that have been crowded
into the valley of Jehoshaphat[1] (i.e. the Kidron
Valley), there are four that stand out from the rest
on account of their architecture. They are known as

[1] According to tradition (Joel 3.2) the Valley of Jehoshaphat is
the valley of judgement. The Jews cover the slopes of the Mount of
Olives and the Mohammedans those of the hill of the Temple.

the tombs of Absalom, of Jehoshaphat, of St James, and of Zechariah[1] (Plate 9).

First, it seems that instead of four vaults there were in reality only two, the monuments being associated in pairs:[2] (Absalom-Jehoshaphat and St James-Zechariah) each mausoleum having its *nephesh* or memorial stele. I shall describe them briefly.

*   *   *

The Tomb of Absalom fig. XVII (fig. XVII, B). This is a cube-shaped monolith hewn out of the cliff-face, some 6 metres wide and 6 m. 50 high, and ornamented with Ionic columns and corner pilasters, supporting an entablature with a Doric frieze surmounted by an 'Egyptian' quirked cornice. Above the entablature the monument was built up with large dressed blocks, forming eventually a cylindrical calotte which was crowned with an ornament in the shape of an inverted chalice, with a cluster of leaves at the top. The total height of this very markedly composite monument was 16 m. 50.

Access into the interior of this curious monument could be gained by descending a staircase of seven unequal steps leading down from an opening in the south face, above the cornice. This brought one into a small, almost square chamber, furnished with a

---

[1] C. Watzinger, *op. cit.*, II, pp. 63–4; *JAT*, I, pp. 331–42; N. Avigad, *Ancient Monuments in the Kidron Valley* (1954).

[2] C. Watzinger, *op. cit.*, p. 63.

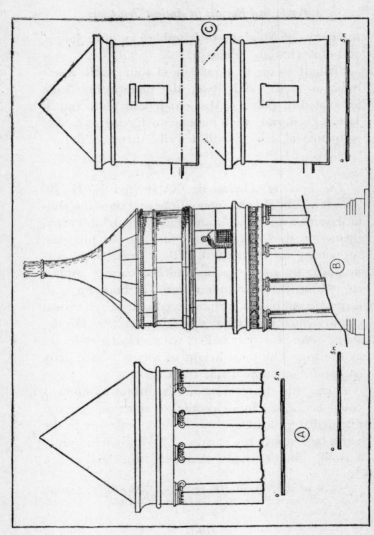

XVII. Tombs of Zechariah and Absalom, and monolith of Siloam (after Vincent and Stève, JAT,

ledge hewn out of the rock. It was thus an individual tomb, but the unusual means of access raises a number of difficulties into which it is not possible to enter here.[1]

The attribution to Absalom is obviously untenable. It was found acceptable only in the sixteenth century, its only foundation being the text in II Samuel 18.18: 'Now Absalom in his life time had taken and reared up for himself the pillar, which is in the king's dale: for he said, I have no son to keep my name in remembrance: and he called the pillar after his own name; and it is called Absalom's monument, unto this day' (R.V.).[2] The strange structure now known as the Tomb of Absalom must always have attracted attention, and it is with no surprise that we read that the Pilgrim of Bordeaux was taken to see it in the year 333. At that time it was thought to be the tomb of Hezekiah, King of Judah, or of his prophet Isaiah.[3]

Completely isolated from the rock-face, this pseudo-tomb of Absalom must certainly be considered as an

[1] It is my opinion that the tomb is of much earlier date than the monument, and that it was only by chance that it happened to be in the portion of rock that was isolated from the cliff for the construction of the monument. If I understand him aright, this opinion appears to be shared by Fr Vincent, *op. cit.*, p. 333. A similar view is put forward by De Vaux in *RB*, 1955, p. 153.

[2] The reading is uncertain, and the Massoretic version is often emended with reference to the Septuagint. Even if it was David who had the monument built for Absalom the point at issue is unaffected. The term used is *yad* (hand), which in any case could very well refer to a stele. [3] Geyer, *op. cit.*, p. 23.

architectural symbol, marking the site of the hypogeum of Jehoshaphat, so-called, the entrance to which is situated in one of the far corners of the small courtyard thus formed.

* * *

The Tomb of Jehoshaphat. Long choked with debris, this was cleared in 1925, and it was then possible to investigate it properly and to draw a plan, which differed in several respects from earlier sketches.[1] It is a true hypogeum (fig. XVIII), containing eight chambers hewn in the rock. The doorway, eight feet wide, opens into a large oblong chamber (A) which gives access to the tomb-chambers. There are two on the east (B, C), one on the north (D), and four on the west, that in the middle (E) having three *kôkîm*, and the other three (F, G, H) having *arcosolium* ledges. Three of the chambers (B, C, H) are provided with small windows opening on to the little courtyard.

One of the most interesting features of the hypogeum is the decoration of the façade, and especially the ornamental triangular pediment (fig. XIX) above the doorway. On either side of a very stylized acanthus in the centre there sprouts a stalk, in whose somewhat stiff convolutions are inserted naturalistic motifs—oranges, lemons, bunches of grapes, and olive

---

[1] Cf., for example, that by Benzinger in *Baedeker, Palestine et Syrie* (1912), and the plan given by Vincent, after Slousch, in *JAT*, I, p. 333, fig. 90.

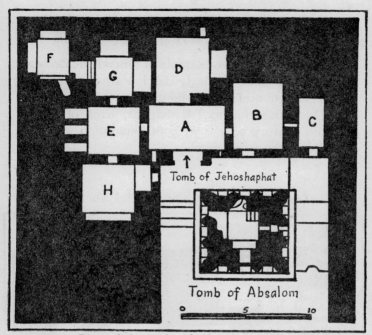

XVIII. *Plan of the tombs of Absalom and Jehoshaphat*
(*ibid., p. 333*)

XIX. *Pediment of the tomb of Jehoshaphat (after Vincent, JAT,*
I, Plate LXXVI)

branches. It is a fine example of syncretistic decoration, conforming to the Jewish law by avoiding the representation of human figures.[1]

The attribution to Jehoshaphat, King of Judah (ninth century B.C.) is without foundation and can no longer be entertained.

*   *   *

The Tomb of St James. This is also an important

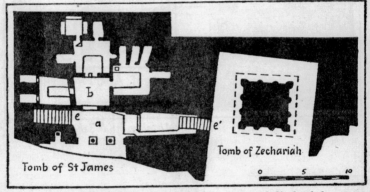

Tomb of Zechariah

Tomb of St James

0   5   10

xx. *Plan of the tombs of St James and Zechariah*
(ibid., *Plate LXXX*)

hypogeum (fig. XX), identifiable, thanks to an inscription, as that of the Bene Hezir family. Hewn entirely out of the rock, this sepulchral group is

[1] There is a reproduction of the tympanum of the Tomb of Jehoshaphat in Vincent, *op. cit.*, Plate LXXVI, a mould of one half of it, presented to the Louvre by De Saulcy (1864), is now in the Sully crypt in the Department of Oriental Antiquities.

distinguished by an imposing porch (*a*), against which there stand out clearly two Doric columns and two corner pilasters. These support a rather plain entablature, the frieze of which is ornamented with triglyphs. From the porch a wide door leads into a large chamber (*b*) comminicating with the tomb-chambers, which contain both *kôkîm* and *arcosolia*.

Two passages lead into the vestibule-porch, one on the north (*e*) and the other on the south (*e'*), the latter being intended to afford communication between the hypogeum and the mausoleum of Zechariah, so-called.[1] That on the north is much easier to negotiate, and leads out into the open.

The inscription carved on the architrave in square Hebrew characters[2] has long puzzled epigraphists, but it is probable that the latest studies have afforded a reading and interpretation which are unlikely to be bettered. This is the translation lately suggested by Fr Vincent:[3]

'This is the tomb and the *nephesh*[4] of Eleazar, Haniah, Jo'azar, Iehudah, Shime'on, Iohannan, the sons of Joseph son of 'Oreb (and also) of Joseph and

[1] See below, p. 92.

[2] A cast given by De Saulcy in 1870 is in the Louvre, in the Sully crypt, Department of Oriental Antiquities.

[3] Vincent, *op. cit.*, p. 336.

[4] The reading of this word, the third in the inscription, is due to N. Avigad. Thanks to it the interpretation given here of the isolated tomb-monuments must henceforward be accepted.

Eleazar the sons of Haniah, priests (of the family) of the Bene Hezir.'[1]

A Hezir is mentioned in I Chronicles 24.15 as the chief of a priestly division dedicated to the service of the Temple. A personage of the same name appears also in the return from the exile, apparently in connection with certain ritual functions (Neh. 10.20). It seems reasonable to suppose that the hypogeum overlooking the Kidron belonged to a priestly family which could claim to be of very ancient descent, and which for centuries had been dedicated to the service of the Temple. Christian tradition appropriated the sepulchre to itself, holding it to be that of St James the Less, the brother of our Lord,[2] martyred not far from that spot, since according to Hegesippus he was thrown down from the 'pinnacle of the Temple' into the valley of the Kidron. What is certain is that the venerable place became the retreat of a hermit, one Epiphanius,[3] thanks to whose directions the 'diligent Anastasius' carried out certain excavations and discovered the bodies of James, Simeon and Zachariah.

*　　*　　*

The Tomb of Zechariah. Like Absalom's monument this is a square monolith cut from the cliff-side (fig. XVII, A). It is 9 metres high, and 5 m. 20 wide, and

[1] For a translation given in 1912, see R. Dussaud, *Les monuments palestiniens et judaïques*, pp. 54–5, with a bibliography.

[2] Mark 6.3; I Cor. 15.7; Gal. 1.19.

[3] Abel, *La sépulture de Saint-Jacques le Mineur*, in *RB*, 1919, p. 499.

is decorated with corner pilasters and Ionic columns and semi-colums. The entablature, which is surmounted by an Egyptian quirked cornice, supports a pyramid which is in one piece with the base. No opening appears anywhere in it, a feature in which it differs completely from the 'monolith of Siloam' (fig. XVII, C), the latter being a tomb 'concerning whose attribution and date widely differing opinions have been expressed.'[1]

It seems to me to be established that the Zechariah monument is the *nephesh* of the Bene Hezir inscription.[2] It must therefore be strictly associated with the neighbouring hypogeum. The connection with Zechariah is another piece of folk-lore—the Christians thought of the son of Barachiah, slain 'between the temple and the altar' (Matt. 23.35),[3] while for the

[1] *JAT*, I, pp. 328–31.

[2] Clermont-Ganneau, as Fr Vincent indicates, has certainly demonstrated in regard to an inscription from Madeba (*RAO*, II, pp. 189–91) that the *nephesh* in association with the tomb represented symbolically 'the actual person of the deceased'. It is however incorrect to say that 'there is a constant and significant relationship between the number of the deceased persons and the number of *nephesh*' (p. 191), for if we reckon the number of the dead in accordance with the number of *loculi* in the hypogeum, then we are clearly mistaken about the significance of the single *nephesh* of the Jehoshaphat and the Bene Hezir mausoleums. It would perhaps be more correct to understand the *nephesh*-monument as representing the family, or the ancestor or the heads of the family (as also in the case of the three pyramids in the 'Tombs of the Kings'; see below, p. 95). In our modern cemeteries we often find, within the family enclosure, the vault containing several tombs, and yet only one monument. This is exactly the same idea.

[3] See *Studies in Biblical Archaeology*, No. 5, *The Temple of Jerusalem*, p. 91, n. 3.

Jews the tomb was that of the son of Jehoiada the priest, slain by Joash (II Chronicles 24.21–2).

Whatever we may think of all these legendary attributions, it is clear that the *four* monuments in the Kidron valley are to be interpreted as *two* sepulchral groups—Absalom-Jehoshaphat and St James-Zechariah. In each case the sepulchre is furnished with a *nephesh*, that is to say a memorial visible to all and set up beside the family vault.[1]

The age of these remains is uncertain, the opinions of the experts being at variance. They are generally thought to belong to the Herodian era, shortly before or shortly after the beginning of the Christian era;[2] but quite recently Fr Vincent had no hesitation in deciding on a date as early as the third century B.C.[3] It seems to me to be beyond doubt that the monuments were in existence during the life of Jesus. I should willingly believe that it was of them He was thinking when, in discourse with the Pharisees towards the end of His earthly life He cried: 'Woe unto you, scribes and Pharisees, hypocrites! because ye build the tombs of the prophets, and garnish the

[1] The same relationship exists in our modern cemeteries between the grave and the vertical grave-stone.

[2] K. Galling, *Die Nekropole*, p. 90; C. Watzinger, *op. cit.*, p. 64; Albright, in *BASOR*, 113 (Feb. 1949), p. 22, n. 62.

[3] Vincent, *op. cit.*, p. 342. E. Will gives a comprehensive survey of this type of funerary monument in *Syria*, XXVI (1949), pp. 258–312. Clearly, the monuments of Absalom and Zechariah must be put side by side with those of Amrith, in Phoenicia (*loc. cit.*, pp. 284–5).

sepulchres of the righteous' (Matt. 23.29). There is also the even more moving thought that as we look at these sepulchres to-day we may be sure that our Lord too saw them on the evening of Maundy Thursday, when after the institution of the Holy Communion 'He went forth with His disciples over the brook Kidron'.[1]

*　　*　　*

The 'Tombs of the Kings'. This hypogeum is situated just short of 725 metres as the crow flies north of the present Damascus Gate, at the side of the road from Jerusalem to Nablus. It was excavated in 1863[2] by De Saulcy, who was persuaded that he had discovered the tombs of the kings of Judah,[3] whence the name by which they have since been known, for the identification at once aroused the most lively controversy. Raoul Rochette, on the other hand, maintained[4] that this was the sepulchre of Helena, Queen of Adiabene,[5]

[1] Gethsemane is only about 300 yards beyond the 'Tomb of Absalom'. Anyone coming from the city must necessarily pass in front of it.

[2] For this date see L. F. Caignart de Saulcy, *Carnets de voyage en Orient* (1843–69), pp. 22 (n. 2), 156, 185, published in 1955 by Fernande Bassan.

[3] De Saulcy, *Voyage en Terre Sainte*, I, pp. 345–410; *Jérusalem*, pp. 224–41.

[4] Raoul Rochette, 'Courtes observations sur les tombeaux des Rois à Jérusalem', in *Revue archéologique*, IX, 1852, pp. 22–37. Rochette paid tribute to all the specialists who, before Saulcy, had studied the sepulchre: Pococke, Niebuhr, Cassas, and Robinson.

[5] A province in the region of the upper Tigris.

who became converted in A.D. 48 to Judaism, together with her son Izates. Another of her sons,
Monobazius, brought their bodies to be buried at
Jerusalem. The Jewish historian Josephus mentions
that the monument, recognizable by its three pyramids, was situated at a distance of three stadia from
the city.[1] The 'pyramids' no longer exist, but the
sepulchre, one of the most imposing of ancient Jerusalem, is in a remarkable state of preservation. Purchased in 1864 by Isaac Pereire, it was given to
France in 1886 by his heirs.

A wide staircase consisting of twenty-four steps cut
in the rock leads to a court, almost square in shape
(26 m. 50 square),[2] itself hewn out of the rock of the
cliff at a depth of from 8 m. 50 to 9 metres.[3] Facing
west, the visitor finds himself in front of a majestic
doorway, 12 metres wide, which opens on to a vestibule, and which is reached by a short flight of steps.
The lintel, supported by two columns with Ionic

[1] *Antiquities*, XX, IV, 3.95. Whatever conclusion one comes to
with regard to the whereabouts of the 'third wall'—the site of the
present wall, or the Sukenik-Mayer line—the distance indicated by
Josephus (555 m.) is incorrect. This however in no way affects the
validity of the identification.

[2] Different authorities give different figures: Benzinger gives
26 m. 50 by 24 m. 50, Dussaud 28 m. by 25 m. 30, and Vincent
20 m. 50 square.

[3] If we add the volume of the staircase, this means that about
7,300 cubic metres of stone had to be hewn out. (For the figures, see
Vincent, *op. cit.*, p. 347, n. 3, with precise details of the irregular
dimensions of the courtyard.)

8. *Jewish tombs on the slopes of the 'Valley of Jehoshaphat'*

9. *Tombs 'of Absalom, St James, and Zechariah'*

10. *Façade of the 'Tombs of the Kings'*

11. *Tombs of the Kings: the stone that is rolled*

capitals,[1] is decorated in bas-relief with a thick garland of foliage interspersed with pomegranates and pine ·cones. The entablature is heightened by a Doric frieze, cut away at the sides, and composed of alternate triglyphs and *paterae*, while in the centre there is a luxuriant bunch of grapes with a crown and a triple palm on either side.[2] Above the frieze is a cornice consisting of a series of projecting ledges.

The entrance to the hypogeum is situated within the vestibule, in its short left-hand side. Here a low door was closed by a stone rolling in a narrow housing[3] (Plate 11). The passage leads to an almost square antechamber whose sides measure about 6 metres communicating with the burial-chambers.

The latter lie to the south and the west, their irregular plan suggesting a series of piecemeal extensions.[4] Moreover, of the seven chambers, two are on a lower level, and one had been so carefully camouflaged that it was missed by the ancient tomb-robbers. It contained a sarcophagus, discovered by De Saulcy on 8th December 1863. On one of the long sides of

[1] See Vincent's reconstruction, *op. cit.*, Plate XXXVIII. Other authorities state that the capitals were Corinthian. Several examples of this type were discovered during the excavation of the courtyard (*ibid.*, Plate XCIV).

[2] A moulding of this frieze was presented to the Louvre by De Saulcy, and is now in the Sully crypt.

[3] This forms one of the finest examples of the stone that was rolled away, mentioned in the Gospels.

[4] Helena's son Izates had had twenty-four sons and twenty-four daughters.

the sarcophagus (fig. XXI) were found two lines of writing, somewhat awkwardly carved, which read first in characters akin to Estranghelo[1] 'Queen Saddan', and then in Aramaic 'Queen Saddah'.[2] Although the body of the queen was found to be

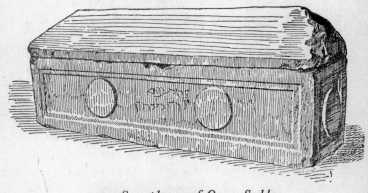

XXI. *Sarcophagus of Queen Saddan*

still in place when the cover was raised, there was but little of it remaining, practically everything having crumbled to dust. Clermont-Ganneau suggested that this Saddan was Helena of Adiabene,[3] and this identification may be considered as almost certainly correct.[4]

[1] *Translator's note*: An archaic form of the Syriac alphabet.

[2] The sarcophagus is in the Louvre. For the mausoleum see Dussaud, *Les monuments palestiniens et judaïques*, pp. 43–4.

[3] Clermont-Ganneau, 'Une nouvelle dédicace à Baal Marcod', in *RAO*, I (1888), p. 107.

[4] For all the reasons, see Vincent, *op. cit.*, pp. 355–6.

The queen was not the only one to have been given a stone coffin. Other sarcophagi, more finely ornamented, were also discovered, or else must have originated from this hypogeum, in which, however, the most usual mode of burial was to place the bodies

XXII. *Sarcophagus from the Tombs of the Kings*

in *kôkîm* or on *arcosolium* ledges. The Louvre possesses several examples[1] bearing most interesting ornamentation of plant and flower designs[2] (fig. XXII).

[1] On view in the Sully crypt. Photographs of these sarcophagi will be found in Dussaud, *op. cit.*, pp. 42–9, and Vincent, *op. cit.*, Plate XCIII.

[2] One of them (*AO*, 5036) is decorated with large single and double rosettes, some of which are enclosed in lilies. On one cover (*AO*, 5057), however, the decoration consists of closely-knit foliated scrolls and garlands, accompanied by a very varied collection of flowers and fruit (lilies, roses, pomegranates, citrons, grapes and acorns) or of different trees (oak, olive). This latter type of ornamentation is clearly the prototype of the decoration found later (second and third centuries A.D.) on lead sarcophagi.

It should be added that whereas the entrance to the hypogeum was, as I have indicated, sealed by means of a rolling millstone, the burial-chambers had stone doors,[1] consisting of heavy and durable stone slabs, turning easily on 'double hinges let into the solid wall'. These measures were taken primarily to protect the bodies against the voracious beasts which frequented the necropolises, for the latter were not hidden from human eyes. Indeed, if we are to believe Josephus, the mausoleum was still marked in his day by three pyramids, which we may doubtless take to be very similar to the 'Tomb of Absalom'.[2]

*   *   *

The Hypogeum of the Herods. Four hundred metres as the crow flies from the south-west corner of the present city wall, in the district that now goes under the name of Nikephurieh, there was discovered in 1892 a subterranean sepulchre (fig. XXIII), which is generally identified with the funerary monument

---

[1] There is an excellent example in the Sully crypt in the Louvre.

[2] For a reconstruction see Vincent *op. cit.*, Plate XCVII. Why *three* pyramids? Was it perhaps in memory of Helena and her two sons, Izates and Monobazius? Such at any rate was the view of Clermont-Ganneau, *RAO*, II (1898), p. 190; the thesis had already been put forward by Raoul Rochette, *loc. cit.*, p. 32. A similar interpretation has been given of the *seven* pyramids set up at Modin on the sepulchre of the Maccabees by Simon, in memory of his father, his mother, and his four brothers, the seventh being for himself (I Mac. 13.28).

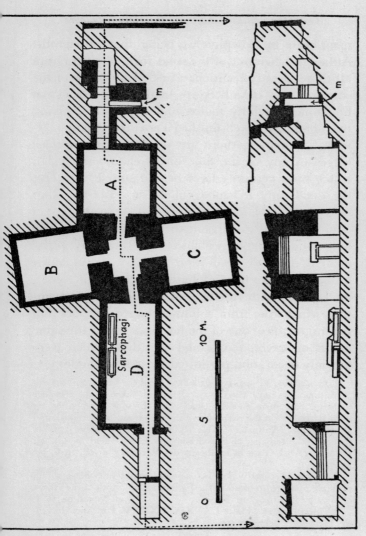

XXIII. *Tombs of the Herods (after Vincent and Steve, JAT, Plate LXXXII)*

mentioned by Josephus as being that of Herod.[1] Although hewn out of the solid rock, it differs from all those already mentioned in that the walls of the corridors and chambers are made of fine blocks of limestone, carefully tooled and dry-jointed, giving the monument a well-finished if not luxurious appearance.[2] Moreover, there are no *kôkîm* or *arcosolium* ledges in any of the four burial-chambers (A–D), which must certainly have been destined to receive the dead only in stone coffins or ossuaries. Two sarcophagi (violated, however) still lay at the foot of one of the walls of the furthest chamber (D). The long trough-shaped coffins[3] were variously ornamented. The sole decoration on one was a moulded frame; the other bore a foliated scroll, its stiff volutes interspersed with rosettes, emanating from an acanthus which rose from a funnel-shaped support. On the fragments of one of the lids were found the same motifs of leaves, scrolls and acanthus, which were the only decoration permitted by strict orthodoxy.[4]

[1] *Jewish War*, V, 507. Nevertheless Herod the Great and several of his sons were not buried there. Herod was taken to the *Herodeion* (between Bethlehem and the Dead Sea); the sons were buried far from Jerusalem, in the *Alexandrion* (Alexander and Aristobulus), and at Hyrcania (Antipater). The sepulchre at Jerusalem possibly sheltered the remains of Herod Agrippa I, who died in A.D. 44. Details in Abel, 'Exils et tombeaux des Hérodes', in *RB*, 1946, pp. 55–74.

[2] A type of construction occasionally found elsewhere, as for example in a Jewish tomb in the Kidron valley, south of the village of Siloam (*RB*, 1925, pp. 255–6).   [3] 1 m. 80 × 0 m. 50.

[4] Vincent, *op. cit.*, Plates LXXXIV–LXXXV. For other decorative themes, see below, p. 106.

One further item should be mentioned: a massive millstone,[1] moving in a narrow housing (*m*), effectively sealed off the hypogeum (fig. XI). This is the second example still to be seen in Jerusalem of the 'stone that was rolled'.

*   *   *

In the other sepulchres in use in our Lord's day or shortly after His death, there is nothing of note which might modify the picture we have of Jewish methods of burial. The so-called 'Tomb of the Judges', which is to be seen on the northern outskirts of Jerusalem, differs from those I have described only in the abundance of its *kôkîm*, arranged in two tiers.[2] The doorway in the façade is ornamented with a triangular pediment decorated with acroteria and a tympanum covered with carvings in very light relief of foliated scrolls and fruit. Above the inner door of the hypogeum the pediment tightly encloses a triple-branched acanthus. This alliance of stylized and naturalistic themes is characteristic of the Alexandrine technique of the first century B.C.[3]

The hypogeum which (quite unwarrantably) goes

[1] Abel, *loc. cit.*, p. 64, gives the dimensions: 1 m. 60 cm. in diameter; 80 cm. thick.

[2] Photograph in Vincent, *op. cit.*, p. 365. There must be nearly sixty of them.

[3] There are mouldings of the façade and of the inner pediment in the Louvre; they were executed by Mauss, the architect, and presented by De Saulcy. For a photograph of the inner pediment, see Dussaud, *op. cit.*, p. 53.

under the name of 'The Apostles' Retreat', [1] is to be seen on the opposite side of Jerusalem, to the south, in the Valley of Hinnom. The façade of the vestibule was decorated with a frieze composed of eight metopes, each bearing a different ornamental motif: [2] several rosettes, garlands, fleurons and bunches of grapes. I shall return to these decorative themes in dealing with the ossuaries which were one of the methods of preserving the bones of the dead in the time of our Lord.

* * *

Ossuaries. From the first century B.C. onwards, Jewish sepulchres are often found to contain small stone coffers holding the bones of one or more bodies. They have been given the name of ossuaries. [3] Of modest dimensions, [4] these boxes were always closed by a lid which was sometimes flat, sometimes like a ridged roof, and sometimes rounded. They perhaps represent an imitation, adapted to Jewish beliefs, of the coffers in which the Romans used to preserve the

[1] A tradition which goes back only to the sixteenth century says that it was in this tomb that the Apostles took refuge after Jesus' arrest in the Garden of Gethsemane.

[2] There is a moulding in the Louvre, presented by De Saulcy. Photograph in Dussaud, *op. cit.*, p. 56. All these mouldings have now the value of originals, since as a result of erosion the original carvings have often either completely perished or suffered considerable damage.

[3] The Greek name is ὀστοφάγος.

[4] Length: 50 cms. to 80 cms.; width: 30 cms. to 80 cms.; height: 25 cms. to 40 cms.

ashes of the dead after cremation. The Jews, who had not adopted this latter custom, inevitably found themselves faced with the problem of a sepulchre in which all the *kôkîm* were occupied. They solved the problem by removing the dry bones from some of the *loculi* and heaping them into these coffers, which would still be kept in the family sepulchre.

These ossuaries are very often ornamented (fig. XXIV), and on them are found some of the motifs of the sarcophagi (especially the rosettes), and also those of the pediments of certain sepulchres (acanthus, for example). The basis of this decoration is both geometrical and naturalistic. The insistance with which the various elements recur indicates that they were recognized as having a symbolic value. There are also numerous ossuaries inscribed with the name or names of the dead, in square Hebrew, Aramaic, or Greek.

It is not my purpose here to give an exhaustive list of this type of monument,[1] but merely to refer to a few examples, taking account of their decoration and of the names carved on them, which naturally often bear some relation to names known to us from biblical sources.

[1] Complete bibliography in Dussaud, *op. cit.*, p. 35; C. Watzinger, *op. cit.*, II, p. 74, n. 2. For Clermont-Ganneau's own work, see *Syria*, IV (19–23), p. 158, n. 6. There is a brief notice by H. Leclercq in *DACL*, XIII, col. 22–7. One would like to see published a complete and detailed study of these monuments, many of which have never been the subject of a published work, and many more only very incompletely dealt with.

The commonest decoration is that in which the rosette occurs. Sometimes plain, sometimes complicated, it is enclosed in a circle (fig. XXIV). The long side of the coffer often includes two rosettes, separated by a vertical band ornamented with one of two wavy ribbons or else a more or less stylized palm-branch. This decoration is worked either simply with a point, or else in light relief, or even sometimes only suggested by a few touches of paint. In some cases incisions and paint are combined.

These common motifs are reproduced and repeated *ad infinitum*. There are many variations: the rosette can be plain or complicated; instead of only two, there may be a line of three or even four; the frame may be composed sometimes of wavy lines, sometimes of diamond checks, zigzags, or nested chalices; sometimes the central motif may be of spreading acanthus leaves (fig. XXV),[1] and sometimes a scarcely stylized palm-tree.[2]

The coffers whose decoration is more complicated in composition are the more noticeable. In some the inspiration behind the ornament is much more imaginative than realistic. A bulky fluted column standing on an ample stepped pedestal supports a

[1] Ossuary from the sepulchre of the sons of Nicanor, Watzinger, *op. cit.*, Plate 30, fig. 70.

[2] Ossuary from the Mount of Olives, *RB*, 1907, p. 412, no. 4 of the plate; sepulchre at Bethphage, *RB*, 1923, p. 256.

XXIV. *Jewish ossuary from a tomb on Mount Scopus*
(after ILN, *29th October 1938, p. 779)*

XXV. *Jewish ossuary from the tomb of the Sons of Nicanor*
(after Watzinger, op. cit., Plate 30)

turreted entablature.[1] What must surely be the most
complicated of these designs is to be seen on an
ossuary (fig. XXVI) which has been re-used in a wall
on the *Via dolorosa* in Jerusalem: three fluted columns
stand on stepped pedestals, that in the centre supporting a palm-branch, and the others supporting
rosettes inscribed in circles, each rosette being flanked
by four umbilicate *paterae*. The spaces between these
columns are occupied by two large segmented figures
contained within circles, and by four semicircles.[2] It
would be interesting to know what abstruse symbolism is concealed in this strange collection.

More simply, other ossuaries reproduce on all four
sides a pattern of bonded masonry,[3] doubtless symbolic of the *domus aeterna* (fig. XXVII), the house of
eternity, the last resting-place of mortal man.

The dead thus laid to rest are not all nameless. It
was in fact a common practice to carve or paint
names, which must certainly have been of those
whose bones, collected together in this way, were
thus receiving a second burial. Among these names
have been found some known from other sources;

[1] *RB*, 1907, p. 411, no. 1 of the plate. Another example, in which
the squat fluted column rests on a three-staged pedestal and is surmounted by a kind of voluted capital, associated with a line of
swastikas, *RB*, 1929, p. 236. Mention is made of others in *BASOR*,
88 (1942), p. 38, but without detailed descriptions.

[2] B. Maisler, 'Art in Herodian Palestine: Tomb Decoration at
Jerusalem', in *ILN*, 29th October 1938, p. 779.

[3] *ILN, ibid.*, p. 779; *RB*, 1923, p. 255; K. Galling, *BRL*, col. 406.

XXVI. *Jewish ossuary (after* ILN, loc. cit.)

XXVII. *Jewish ossuary* (ibid.)

and others have sometimes been wrongly read, and, as I shall indicate later, with sensational results!

One of the most famous collections of ossuaries was that discovered on the eastern slope of the Mount of Olives, at Bethphage. It had belonged to the sons of Nicanor,[1] an Alexandrine Jew whose fame rests upon his having donated one of the most beautiful of the bronze Temple gates at Jerusalem.[2]

In 1873 a hypogeum excavated on the Mount of Offence, south-east of Jerusalem, had already produced a certain number of ossuaries inscribed in Hebrew and Greek, furnishing an interesting list of names.[3] In Hebrew there appeared Salome, Judah the Scribe, Simeon son of Jesus, Martha, Eleazar (=Lazarus), Shalamsion, daughter of Simeon the Priest; and in Greek, Jesus, Nathaniel, Hedaea,

---

[1] *RB*, 1900, pp. 106–12. An ossuary inscribed with the same names was studied from clay impressions and photographs, some years later, by Clermont-Ganneau, 'La "Porte de Nicanor" du Temple de Jérusalem', in *RAO*, V (1903), pp. 334–40. The bilingual text ran, in Greek: 'Bones of [the family] of Nicanor the Alexandrine, who made the gates', and in Hebrew: 'Niqanor Alacsa'. The exact position of the sepulchre was not given by Miss Dickson, who possessed the ossuary. K. Galling, *BRL*, col. 405, proposes a different reading, believing that a slip had been made by the engraver. This would give the reading: 'Bones of Nicanor the Alexandrine' (not Οστα των, but Οστατου).

[2] 'Nicanor's gate' was between the Women's Court and the Court of Israel. According to tradition it was 50 cubits (25 m.) high, and 40 cubits (20 m.) wide. It required at least twenty men to turn it on its hinges. Its leaves, of Corinthian bronze, were overlaid with gold and silver. For the site of this gate, see *Studies in Biblical Archaeology*, No. 5, *The Temple of Jerusalem*, pp. 89–90.

[3] Clermont-Ganneau, in *PEFQS*, 1874, pp. 7–10.

Kythras, Moschas, and Mary. The name of Jesus, mentioned three times, was twice followed by a cross.[1] It was, to say the least, a bold conclusion to claim that this was the family tomb of Mary, Martha and Lazarus of Bethany—and even more so to associate Jesus with them, especially since references to three persons of this name were found in the same vault.

A similarly negative appreciation must be made with regard to an ossuary around which a great controversy raged a quarter of a century ago. It had been mentioned and commented upon by Sukenik in the course of a communication presented by him on 6th January, 1931, before the Deutsche Archaeologische Gesellschaft of Berlin.[2] The coffer bore on one of its long sides an Aramaic inscription which read: 'Jesus son of Joseph.' One can guess the startling conclusion that had been arrived at; it called forth a lively and pertinent reply from Fr Vincent,[3] who had no difficulty in showing that it was no more than a coincidence, due to the extreme frequency in Palestine of the names Joseph and Jesus.

It has been established that an ossuary might contain the bones either of one individual or of

---

[1] Did the sign of the cross, found, moreover, also after the name of Judah, mean that these were Christians? The question deserves an answer, and I shall deal with it further on.

[2] E. L. Sukenik, *Jüdische Gräber Jerusalems und Christi Geburt.*

[3] Vincent, 'Jésus fils de Josèphe', in *Rendiconti della Pontificia Accademia Romana di Archaeologia*, VII (1932), pp. 215-39.

several. There have also been found, for example, couples (Eleazar and his wife; [1] Mary and Johanan [2]), a mother and son (Shalom and Mattiah her son [3]), a father and son (Simeon the elder and Joseph his son [4]), children (the sons of Nicanor, the sons of Eleazar, the sons of Hanan [5]). Sometimes a whole family is gathered together in the same coffer, since six names, some feminine (Salome, Mariam), and some masculine (Eliezer, Joseph) are found inscribed on an ossuary from a sepulchre at Siloam. [6]

In the case of individual reinterments we find both men and women, sometimes referred to by their 'first name' only, and sometimes with an indication of descent—'son of . . .', 'daughter of . . .'—or of conjugal dependence—'wife of . . .'. Sometimes the place of origin or domicile is given—'Judah son of Judah, of Bethel', 'Mary, wife of Alexander of Capua'. [7] Children may evoke implicitly their filial attachment—'Shalamsion, our mother', [8] 'Dositheos, our father', with, in this last case, the warning 'And not to be opened'. [9]

*   *   *

[1] *RB*, 1904, p. 263; Cl.-Ganneau, *RAO*, VI, 211.
[2] *RB*, 1907, p. 412. It is not impossible that Mary was the daughter, and not the wife, of Johanan.   [3] *RB*, 1929, p. 234.
[4] *RB*, 1925, p. 259. One should avoid the suggestion that this 'Simeon the elder' is to be identified with the old man Simeon in Luke 2.25.   [5] *RB*, 1929, p. 235.
[6] Sukenik, in *BASOR*, 88 (1942), p. 38, where only four names are specified.   [7] *RB*, 1902, pp. 104–6.   [8] *RB*, 1929, p. 233.
[9] *RB*, 1929, p. 231. A similar warning appears on the slab bearing the name of Uzziah, King of Judah (781–740 B.C.), whose body was

This rapid survey[1] may fittingly be terminated by a reference to a more recent discovery, and one which occasioned something of a sensation at the time. In September 1945 a rock-tomb was excavated in the suburb of Talpioth not far from the road from Jerusalem to Bethlehem. Hewn out of the solid cliff (fig. XXVIII), it contains five *loculi* of the *kôkîm* type, arranged on various levels. Sukenik and Avigad, who directed the work, found eleven ossuaries.[2] Some of them are decorated with incised patterns (rosettes and more or less stylized plants), and are directly related to the series I have already described. Five bear inscriptions—three in Aramaic and two in Greek. The first three present no difficulty, it being easy to

---

certainly reinterred several hundred years after his death: 'Here have been laid the bones of Uzziah, King of Judah. Not to be opened!' There is an excellent photograph of the slab in E. L. Sukenik, *Megillôt Genouzôt*, Plate IV. This stone, unfortunately not *in situ*, was discovered by Sukenik among the collections of the Russian Convent on the Mount of Olives, and is the subject of notices by him in *PEFQS*, 1931, pp. 217–21; 1932, pp. 106–7. The script of the text engraved on the copper scrolls from Qumran is similar to that of the letters on the Uzziah slab. (See *RB*, 1954, p. 196.)

[1] I would repeat that my aim in this section has been confined to giving a general view of this type of monument, mentioning only those aspects which have a bearing on the Bible. I have omitted to deal with the two lids from Bethphage, for even if they are authentic (Fr Vincent has questioned their authenticity, *RB*, 1924, p. 473), they furnish workmen's accounts, and have no direct connection with our subject. For these lids, see Dussaud, in *Syria*, IV (1923), pp. 241–9; V (1924), pp. 388–9; P. G. Orfali, in *RB*, 1924, pp. 253–60.

[2] E. L. Sukenik, 'The Earliest Records of Christianity', in *AJA*, LI (1947), pp. 351–65. To these eleven ossuaries must be added three others which were found before the official excavation.

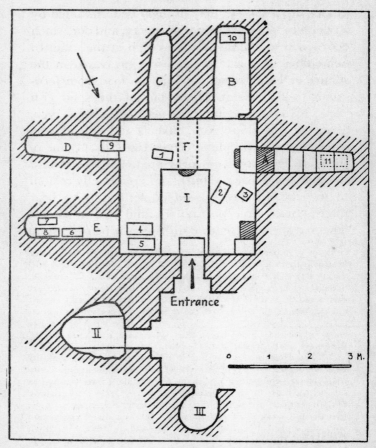

XXVIII. *Jewish sepulchre at Talpioth (after* AJA, *LI, 1947,*
p. 353)

read the names: Simeon Barsaba; Miriam daughter of Simeon; Mat' (abbreviated form of Mattathias). The two Greek inscriptions (fig. XXIX) are harder to interpret. There is no doubt at all that the name of Jesus (*Iesous*) appears, followed once by the word

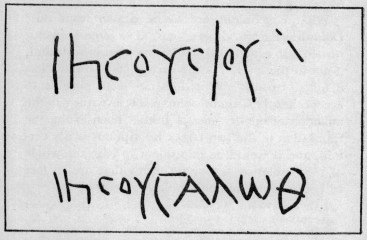

XXIX. *Graffiti in the Talpioth sepulchre* (ibid., *p. 358*)

iou, and once by *alōth*. Having stated very fairly the obscurities present in the terminology, Sukenik goes on to state that in his estimation we have here a reference to Jesus, and that His name, which appears twice, is followed by an exclamation which, when considered in the light of Greek funerary epitaphs, probably invoked the idea of misfortune or lamentation.

Lastly it must be mentioned that a number of ossuaries bear, either carved in the stone, or else marked with charcoal or paint, a sign which is incontestably a cross. As we saw above, it had already been observed on some of the ossuaries from the Mount of Offence.

What conclusions are to be drawn from this? Doubtless the world press[1] has, as so often happens, turned into categorical statements what in the mind, if not in the mouth, of the excavator was much less definite. In any case it does not seem possible to accept that the Talpioth ossuaries bear witness to the affliction of the disciples of Jesus.[2] Then again, the translation of the two Greek inscriptions is not certain, and it would be imprudent to base the whole of the desolation theory on terms that are in fact still obscure and of doubtful interpretation.[3]

[1] *New York Times*, 3rd October 1945; *Daily Herald*, 3rd October 1945; *France-Soir*, 11th October 1945.

[2] An agency dispatch read as follows: 'According to the preliminary investigations made by the archaeologists, it seems that these texts are connected with the drama of Calvary, and that they were actually written by an eye-witness on the morrow of the Crucifixion, being in fact lamentations by Jewish disciples for Christ's death.' The French Archaeological School at Jerusalem protested shortly afterwards against the 'unreasonable publicity' accorded to this discovery, in consequence of which Mr Hamilton, the Director of Palestine Antiquities, issued a joint statement with Dr Sukenik to the effect that before a scientific study of the tomb and its contents had been made 'it would be premature to admit any relationship between this tomb and any event or person known from Holy Scripture', *CRA*, 1945, 30th October, pp. 518–19.

[3] See the study of this problem by Sukenik in *AJA*, LI, p. 362. It is possible that 'Ιησοῦς ἰού ought to be translated 'Jesus (son of)

On the other hand, I am less sceptical about the sign of the cross, carved, painted, or marked in charcoal, found at Talpioth and elsewhere. It had always been thought that the cross (which, it may be added, appears as an ornamental and symbolic motif from the very earliest times, in Mesopotamia and Persia) had only come to be used as a Christian symbol at a very late date, and never before the second century. There was a cross carved in relief on the wall of a house in Pompeii, which was the subject of much controversy; but together with Professor A. Maiuri *I myself saw*, in the Casa del Bicentennario at Herculaneum, the marks which I personally have no doubt were left by a cross hung in a private oratory.[1] I therefore consider it to be proved that the cross was, in the West, used as a Christian symbol from the fourth quarter of the first century, at the latest.[2] Of course that does not mean that the same is true of the East, or, specifically, of Jerusalem; but if one refuses to accept the fact of its symbolic use at that

Jehu'. But if $\dot{a}\lambda\dot{\omega}\theta$ transcribes the Hebrew word meaning aloe (Hamilton Communiqué, *CRA*, *loc. cit.*, p. 519), one is left wondering what that might signify in the present context!

[1] Thus I find myself in agreement with the interpretation given by A. Maiuri, 'La croce di Ercolano', in *Rendiconti dell'Accademia di Archeologia Romana*, 1939, pp. 193–218, which, however, is contested by J. Carcopino, *Etudes d'histoire chrétienne*, p. 49. For a photograph of the imprint of the Herculaneum cross, see *AJA*, LI, Plate LXXXVIII.

[2] Herculaneum, it will be remembered, was destroyed by an eruption of Mount Vesuvius in A.D. 79.

time, it is going to be—and has been found[1]—difficult to explain the significance of these unmistakable signs.[2]

It should be mentioned also that the name Barsabas, carved on one of the ossuaries, is found only here and in the New Testament (Acts 1.23; 15.22); and that there was picked up in the tomb a coin of Agrippa I,[3] bearing the date of the sixth year of that king's reign, i.e. A.D. 42–3.

We know that two tendencies rapidly became apparent in the primitive Church: the Jewish Christians, who claimed to follow James, Peter and John (Gal. 2.9), and the Gentile Christians, who considered themselves the spiritual children of Paul. The Jerusalem Christians retained as much of Judaism as was compatible with the new faith. Who can deny that the Talpioth sepulchre is an illustration of this fact, at least so far as funerary rites are concerned? In fact, these new converts must have followed the customs of Jewish burial. They retained their ancestors' and compatriots' ossuaries, the decoration of

[1] See, for example, C. H. Kraeling in *BA*, IX (1946), p. 20.

[2] Sukenik does not omit to mention Clermont-Ganneau's opinion concerning the ossuaries marked with a cross which were discovered in 1873 in the sepulchre on the Mount of Offence (see above, p. 111). According to the French orientalist, whose extraordinary sureness of touch in diagnoses of this sort was universally recognized, an interpretation in terms of Christian symbolism could not be entirely excluded. 'In one way or another,' he wrote, 'the new doctrine must have found its way inside the Jewish system.' See Clermont-Ganneau, *Archaeological Researches in Palestine*, I (1899), pp. 381 ff.

[3] King Herod of Acts 12.1.

which did not and could not offend them, but in certain cases they added a sign—the cross, which marked the essential difference between the Law of Moses and the New Covenant.[1] That is why, all things considered, it is not impossible in my opinion that archaeology has given us, not indeed a disconsolate commentary on the drama of Good Friday, but perhaps the earliest evidence for the presence in Jerusalem of the first Christian community.

*   *   *

This interpretation, put forward by me some years ago,[2] and still adhered to while this Study was in preparation,[3] appears likely to receive startling confirmation as a result of some quite recent discoveries.[4]

In the *Dominus flevit*, a Franciscan property on the slopes of the Mount of Olives, a cemetery has just

[1] In connection with a similar and more recent discovery, referred to below, I find (*RB*, 1954, p. 569) an appreciation couched in terms almost identical with my own. It is worth quoting: 'That there was a Christian community in Jerusalem in the first century is certain, and there is nothing surprising in the discovery of graves of its members, just as it is very natural that these first brethren should have marked their new faith by some sign which distinguished them from the rest of the Jews.' I had not seen this article when I wrote. See below.

[2] *Le Christianisme au XXᵉ siecle*, 2nd June 1949.

[3] In July 1954.

[4] They appear in an 'Archaeological chronicle' printed in *RB*, 1954, pp. 568–70, which came to my notice only in February 1955 after my return from Mari, when what I had written above was already in the press.

been discovered which appears to be of the greatest importance. Though many of the tombs go back only to the Byzantine period and consequently have only a relatively slight bearing on our inquiry, others can be dated, without any possible doubt, as belonging to the 'Herodian' period, i.e. the first century A.D. There are not only burials of the *kôkîm* type, but what is more—numerous ossuaries, many of them bearing inscriptions.

Fr Bagatti, the Franciscan brother who explored this cemetery, has published the results of his investigation, and the more important of his observations.[1] Among the names which he found written in either Aramaic or Greek, some carved and some inscribed in charcoal, he notes several which recur in the Gospels: Jairus (Mark 5.22; Luke 8.41), Salome (Mark 15.40; 16.1), Martha, Mary, Simon son of Jonas (Matt. 16.17).

It is impossible in the present state of our knowledge to know whether the people who bore these names are the same as those mentioned in the Gospels. There remains a gap that is not easy to bridge—but coincidences of this sort are none the less striking.

If, therefore, we cannot prove that the ossuaries

[1] Bellarmino Bagatti, 'Scoperta di un cimitero giudeo-cristiano al "Dominus flevit",' *Studii Biblici Franciscani*, Liber Annus III (1952–3), pp. 149–84, Jerusalem. I owe this information and the reference to *RB*, 1954, p. 568, n. 1, the Italian publication being otherwise inaccessible to me.

discovered housed the mortal remains of biblical personages, it does henceforward appear pratically certain that the dead to whom these inscriptions bear witness were Christians, for the following reasons. There was noticed on the ossuary of one 'Judah the proselyte of Tyre' a 'Constantinian' monogram. This sign had not previously been thought so ancient. Another combination of three letters, I, X, B, can scarcely be read as meaning anything other than *Iesous, Christos, Basileus* (i.e. Jesus Christ King). Lastly, there is a very carefully-drawn cross reminiscent of those already found at Talpioth and on the Mount of Offence.

Similarly, while investigating the Jewish cemetery of Sanhedriah, north of Jerusalem, J. J. Rotschild noted crosses on three tombs. He attributes them also to Jewish Christians, who probably carved them between the middle of the second and the middle of the third centuries as a mark of their new faith.[1]

All this mass of evidence can hardly lead to any other conclusion.[2] On all sides there is increasing evidence of the presence in Jerusalem of the Christian community whose rapid growth from the Day of Pentecost onwards is reported in the biblical tradition of the Acts of the Apostles.

[1] *PEQ*, LXXXVI, 1954, pp. 17–20. This reference is likewise given in *RB*, 1954, p. 570, n. 1.

[2] 'One cannot fail to recognize the extreme importance of this discovery, if the cautious but positive and well-documented interpretation of Fr Bagatti proves to be correct,' *RB*, 1954, pp. 569–70.

It makes a fitting sequel, not only to the tragedy of Golgotha, but also—and above all—to the drama of the empty Tomb on Easter morning.

BIBLIOGRAPHY

It would be out of the question to give an exhaustive bibliography of a subject which has inspired innumerable books and articles; nor is it necessary for me to recapitulate here the titles of all the works I have used which appear in the footnotes to this study. My intention is to indicate only those works which are essential to each aspect of the problem, and on which I myself have relied. The specialist reader who wishes to go more deeply into the subject will find that they furnish a much more comprehensive documentation, together with all the references he could desire.

GENERAL WORKS

The two basic works are those forming part of the comprehensive series edited by the Dominican Fathers of Jerusalem:

L. H. Vincent and F. M. Abel, *Jérusalem. Recherches de topographie, d'archéologie et d'histoire*. Vol. 2: *Jérusalem nouvelle*, Pts. I and II (1914), 'Aelia Capitolina', 'Le Saint-Sépulcre', pp. 1–300.

L. H. Vincent, *Jérusalem de l'Ancien Testament*, I, Paris, 1954, with maps and drawings by A. M. Stève.

Bibliography

For the problem of the Church of the Holy Sepulchre, the very important monograph by J. Jeremias, *Golgotha*, Leipzig, 1926, and a valuable chapter in G. H. Dalman, *Sacred Sites and Ways*, S.P.C.K., London, 1935, pp. 346–81. It is also advisable to compare the older theories with the new interpretations suggested by Andrei Grabar in *Martyrium. Recherches sur le culte des reliques et l'art chrétien antique*, Paris, 1946. See also the thesis for the Baccalaureate in Theology of the Faculty of Protestant Theology in Paris, by Albert Finet, *L'emplacement du Calvaire et du Saint-Sépulchre* (1928), and the study by E. T. Richmond, *The Sites of the Crucifixion and the Resurrection* (1934).

More concise information will be found in the following handbooks:

A. G. Barrois, *Manuel d'archéologie biblique*, II, 1935, pp. 299–312, 314–17 (burials, sepulchres, ossuaries, tomb of Jesus).

K. Galling, *Biblisches Reallexikon*, Tübingen, 1937, articles, *Grab, Ossuar, Sarkophag*.

C. Watzinger, *Denkmäler Palästinas*, Leipzig, 1935, pp. 59–76 (burials); pp. 117–20 (Constantinian Church of the Holy Sepulchre).

For the historical background:

F. M. Abel, *Histoire de la Palestine*, II, 1952, pp. 102–4 (Hadrian's policy); pp. 267–70 (Constantine's buildings).

The various guide books to Palestine may also be

consulted with profit. Being edited by experts they are often authoritative. For example:

Palestine et Syrie (Baedeker. Benzinger's revision).

Syrie-Palestine (Guides Bleus. Text by Abel).

While the innumerable modern travel-books tell us little of the ancient history of the sites, there is on the other hand much to be gleaned from the accounts of ancient travellers, who in many cases saw the monuments in a much better state of preservation than is now possible.

The texts of the accounts by early pilgrims will be found in Vincent-Abel, *Jérusalem*: The Bordeaux Pilgrim, fourth century A.D. (p. 208); Ætheria, end of the fourth century (pp. 210–14); the anonymous pilgrim of Placentia, *c*. A.D. 570 (p. 216); Arculf, A.D. 670 (pp. 233–4); Willibald, A.D. 724 (p. 234). All these and many more appear in the invaluable collection by Geyer, *Itinera Hierosolymitana saeculi iiii–viii*, Corpus Scriptorum Ecclesiasticorum Latinorum, 1898. English texts will be found in the various volumes of the *Library of the Palestine Pilgrims' Text Society*, 1897. It may be taken that later accounts are largely copies of the earlier writings.

Among the works that appeared during the last century the following are worthy of mention:

Vogüé (Marquis de), *Les Eglises de Terre Sainte*, 1860.

F. de Saulcy, *Voyage en Terre Sainte*, 1864; *Jérusalem*, 1882 (in spite of extravagances and flagrant errors in identification—for example, the 'Tombs of the

Kings', identified by him as being those of the Kings of Judah, pp. 224–41).

V. Guérin, *La Terre Sainte*, I, 1882, pp. 96–112, with noteworthy illustrations, intended for the edification of the general public, but based on a thorough knowledge of the country, which is also evident in his *Description géographique, historique et archéologique de la Palestine*, in 7 vols., 1868–80.

E. Robinson, *Biblical Researches in Palestine*, 1856.

The collection *Die Palästina-Literatur*, under the general direction of Peter Thomsen, gives an exhaustive list of all works dealing with Palestine, but unfortunately without discrimination in the matter of their individual worth. As far as concerns publications that have appeared since 1925 and which have a bearing on this study, the references are as follows:

Church of the Holy Sepulchre: V, 2, pp. 365–6; 3, pp. 547, 550–1; VI, 2, pp. 384–5, 529.

Relics of the Passion: V, 2, pp. 251–2; VI, 1, pp. 273–5.

Legends, Adam, Melchisedek: V, 3, p. 549.

Earliest pilgrims to Jerusalem: V, 3, p. 553.

The 'third wall': V, 3, p. 495.

Excavations at the 'Tomb of Jehoshaphat': V, 3, p. 498.

Ossuaries: V, 6, pp. 398–400, 414–15, 419; 3, pp. 469, 497–8.

Ossuary of 'Jesus son of Joseph': with an extensive bibliography of the controversy: V, 2, p. 419.

Ossuary of Nicanor: V, 2, p. 438.

Slab of King Uzziah: V, 2, p. 414.

ABBREVIATIONS

SPECIALIST REVIEWS

It is necessary to refer constantly to the Palestinian and Orientalist reviews, which record discoveries year by year. The most important are:

RB: *Revue Biblique.*
JPOS: *Journal of the Palestine Oriental Society.*
PEFQS: *Palestine Exploration Fund Quarterly Statement.*
QDAP: *Quarterly of the Department of Antiquities in Palestine.*
BASOR: *Bulletin of the American Schools of Oriental Research.*
BA: *The Biblical Archaeologist.*
ILN: *Illustrated London News.*
IEJ: *Israel Exploration Journal.*
JJPES: *Journal of the Jewish Palestine Exploration Society.*
PJB: *Palästina Jahrbuch.*
ZDMG: *Zeitschrift der Deutschen Morgenländischen Gesellschaft.*
ZDPV: *Zeitschrift des Deutschen Palästinavereins.*

Date Due